I0211175

WARM SOCKS

WARM SOCKS

Life Lessons from My Father

By
Edna Brown Mark

RESOURCE *Publications* · Eugene, Oregon

WARM SOCKS
Life Lessons from My Father

Copyright © 2021 Edna Brown Mark. All rights reserved. Except for brief quotations in critical publications or reviews, no part of this book may be reproduced in any manner without prior written permission from the publisher. Write: Permissions, Wipf and Stock Publishers, 199 W. 8th Ave., Suite 3, Eugene, OR 97401.

Resource Publications
An Imprint of Wipf and Stock Publishers
199 W. 8th Ave., Suite 3
Eugene, OR 97401

www.wipfandstock.com

PAPERBACK ISBN: 978-1-6667-1012-0
HARDCOVER ISBN: 978-1-6667-1013-7
EBOOK ISBN: 978-1-6667-1014-4

All Scripture quotations are from The Authorized (King James) Version. Rights in the Authorized Version in the United Kingdom are vested in the Crown. Reproduced by permission of the Crown's patentee, Cambridge University Press.

08/04/21

This book is dedicated to my brother, Daniel Chester Hunter Brown, who was two weeks old when Daddy died. May this story give you a better understanding of who our father was.

Train up a child in the way he should go,
even when he is old he will not depart from it.

—PROVERBS 22:16 (KJV)

Contents

Acknowledgement | ix

1 Stranger in Distress | 1

2 Life's Greatest Gift | 13

3 Daddy's Good Book | 18

4 Coming Home Late | 25

5 A Wholesome Tongue | 29

6 Warm Socks | 33

7 One Side of a Story | 37

8 Aunt Katie's Butter Cookies | 40

9 Fried Fish And Buttermilk Biscuits | 44

10 He'll Be Home Soon | 51

11 Forgiving Miss Clara | 57

12 Centraneta | 65

13 Thanksgiving Guest | 78

14 Jesus's Birthday Celebration | 90

15 Fear Not | 94

16 Farm Work Isn't for Me | 100

17 Church Folks | 109

18 Honor Your Father and Mother | 114

19 Black Patent Shoes | 121

20 Something Is Wrong | 126

21 Goodbye, Sweet Daddy | 131

22 It's What He Taught Me | 143

Endnotes | 148

Acknowledgement

I am grateful to my parents, Berkeley Herbert and Willie Elizabeth Brown, for their love, support, guidance, and essential life-skills teaching.

Special thanks to Doris Brown, Linda Blackmon, Fanchon Leath, Angela Lewis, and Betty Saul for taking time out of their busy schedules to read my manuscript. Your honesty, suggestions, and advice helped me refine my ideas and approach throughout this process.

Special recognition to Walter Preston Leath Jr., Daryl Leath, Danny Brown, Ebony Leath, and Natalie Leath for believing in me. Your belief in me kept me going through the periods of self-doubt, setbacks, and uncertainty. This book would not have been possible without you.

I am eternally grateful to Wipf and Stock and the team for taking a chance on me, and welcoming me to the Wipf and Stock family.

Above all, thank you, Great Almighty God, the author of knowledge and wisdom, for your countless love.

1

Stranger in Distress

I once thought life was unfair and difficult, but as I grew older I realized that life is what you make it. God created me and a wonderful world to live in, and it was up to me how I was going to live my life. He gave me a sound mind, health, strength, loving Christian parents, shelter, food, clothing, and a purpose. Even though my parents raised me in church, I stopped going at the age of eighteen. I prayed, but my prayers were selfish. As a child, teenager, and young adult I didn't realize the value of the gift God had given me. I wanted to be like other people, even though I didn't know anything about them. Just because they had a big house, name-brand clothing, successful careers, wealth, and fancy cars I thought they had everything. I didn't realize during my younger years that material things distract from life's purpose, and the sense of purpose fades over time. In the 1950s, husbands were the sole providers for their families, and their wives were humble and expected their husbands to take charge regardless of the circumstance. My mother was one of those women. Since Daddy had the responsibility of taking care of us, I felt he hadn't fulfilled his role as a provider because I didn't get the things I wanted as a child. During different stages of my life, I felt strongly that not having had materials things as a child influenced my emotional reactions later in my life. After listening and communicating with many "influential people" who aspired to have more in life, it took one stranger to make me clearly see that money or material things can't buy happiness. For the first time I realized that Daddy had fulfilled his role by giving me everything I needed to maintain a healthy and happy existence. After meeting the stranger, instantly my challenges were replaced with an appreciation of the gifts God had given me from the minute I was born. It was right in front of me but I had overlooked it because I was too busy looking at things that prevented me from recognizing God's unfailing love. I had disregarded the Bible verse 1 John 2:16–17, which was preached so many times in church: "For all that is in the world, the lust of the flesh, and the lust of the eyes, and the pride of life, is not of the Father, but is of the world. And the world passeth away, and the lust thereof: but he that doeth the will of God abideth forever."

A week off didn't come easy at my stressful job. I had put in several requests for a vacation and they were denied because of the demands of the Internal Medicine Clinic, and we were understaffed. When time off was finally approved, I decided to pamper myself the entire week with activities to relax and reduce my stress. One of the items on my list was a warm bubble bath to help improve my health and mental well-being. My legs were aching from standing up most of the day at my job, and my muscles were tense. I had purchased my favorite bath products, essential oils, and a bottle of aged red wine. I placed lit candles on each corner of the bathtub and Barry White's greatest hits were playing in the background. I had just sat down in the tub and took a sip of my Merlot red wine when the telephone rang. I ignored it, took another sip of wine, and lip-synced Barry White's song "Can't Get Enough of Your Love." The telephone continued to ring repeatedly. The caller was determined to keep ringing my telephone until I picked it up. I felt it was an emergency because of the continuous rings.

"Hello Joann. Is everything okay?"

"My car wouldn't start this morning. I had it towed in. The mechanic just called me and told me the motor is gone. It's going to cost me a fortune to have them replace the motor and I don't have it. I can't believe this happened when I don't have a job to pay for the repairs."

"I'm so sorry, Joann."

"The reason I'm calling is that I have an internal medicine appointment in two hours and I have no way to get there. I don't want to reschedule my appointment because I'm almost out of my blood pressure pills. Do you mind taking me? I don't know anyone else to call."

"Okay, I will pick you up in an hour."

"Thank you so much, Edna. I'm sorry if I ruined your day. I know you had plans for your vacation."

"Don't worry about it. You don't need to stress out and get your blood pressure out of control."

"I don't know what I would do without you."

I was so angry my relaxing day was over, but I knew the right thing to do was to take Joann to her appointment. I met Joann twenty years ago standing in line at 4:00 a.m. to purchase a Christmas gift at a Sears Black Friday sale. The wait was long enough for us to learn about each other and we became friends instantly. After purchasing our gifts at Sears, we decided to shop all day and have lunch together. At the end of the day we exchanged telephone numbers, and we have been close friends ever since that day. She's a good listener and is trustworthy, selfless, forgiving, nonjudgmental, and caring. She is also my personal advisor. She has no family nearby and doesn't have skills or experience to get a high- or average-paying job to support herself. She has worked hard all her life in fast-food restaurants as a cook with a little-above-minimum wage.

We arrived just in time for Joann's appointment and she was called back to the nurse's station immediately after checking in. After a waiting-room chair became available, I sat down and began reading *Women and Stress, A Practical Approach to Managing Tension* by Jean Lush and Pam Vredevelt. I had problems managing my stress and after no success, I attended a stress management class. My instructor recommended the book to me and several of my colleagues who also attended the class. We were reassured that the book would help us manage stress in healthy and productive ways. I was determined to read every page. Reading this book was one of the things I had promised myself to do while I was on vacation. Just like my bubble baths, my reading was interrupted. This time, I interrupted myself from reading because of a strange and uneasy feeling. Close to where I was seated, I immediately noticed a young woman standing against the wall in the hallway near an examination room. Her tall, lean body, striking beauty, sparkling diamond earrings, and wide-band diamond bracelet captured my attention. She was wearing a short-sleeved, metallic, royal-blue, button-front top; charcoal stretch-knit trousers that flattered her perfectly-shaped, slim figure; and chunky, charcoal, leather, three-inch, heel-knotted slide sandals. Her hair was brown and nourished, and it complimented her oval-shaped face. Her toenails and fingernails were professionally polished metallic blue with wildflower designs. The mild scent of her perfume spread throughout the clinic, and her pinned-up, victory-rolls hairstyle gave her sex appeal. It was obvious that she was wealthy and doleful.

I heard her softly sniffing and sobbing, and instantly I wanted to comfort her. She was trying to prevent the tears from running down her face by wiping them off with her hands. She wasn't doing a good job. Even though she had smeared her eyeliner and makeup, it didn't take away from her beauty. Ambivalently, I grabbed some tissues from the waiting-room table and slowly walked over to her. I gave her the tissues, afraid I had made a mistake by interfering in a private matter that was none of my business. I turned around to go back to my seat, but I couldn't leave her that way. I started a conversation with her.

"Are you alright?"

"I'm fine."

Her answer didn't convince me. I asked her again to make sure I felt comfortable enough to leave her alone.

"Are you sure?"

"Yes, I'm sure."

"I'm more than happy to get you something to eat or drink."

"Thank you, but I'm not hungry or thirsty."

"If you need immediate service, I can get a nurse for you."

"Oh no. I'm not here to be seen."

"Are you with a friend or family member?"

"Yes."

"Do you need to talk to someone?"

"Not really."

"I know it's hard talking to someone you don't know, but I'm willing to listen."

"I appreciate your willingness to listen, but I'm embarrassed to talk about my personal problems to anyone."

"Holding things inside isn't healthy. Find someone you can trust to talk to. I just met you and I can tell you're a sweet and caring person. Whatever is bothering you, don't let it get the best of you."

"It's difficult."

"I understand. If you need to talk, know that I'm willing to listen. I won't judge or ridicule you."

She smiled at me and immediately began telling me her story.

"I brought my father to the clinic for a follow-up appointment and while we were waiting, he collapsed to the floor. The medical staff gave him cardiopulmonary resuscitation and they were able to save him. Dr. Peterson said he will have to admit him to the hospital because he had a heart attack. He said further tests are needed to treat him appropriately. I have his room number but I'm waiting for Mother to pick me up. I'm going with her to see Father in his room. It has been a terrible day. I'm tired and I don't feel like driving back home."

"I'm very sorry." I hope he has a speedy recovery. I know it must be hard on you and your family."

The next sentence that came out of her mouth disturbed me.

"Unfortunately, I'm not sorry and I wouldn't care if he never comes back home. Mother and I would be so much better off without him. He is toxic and an emotionally broken man. I'm crying because I'm exhausted and frustrated with pretending to be a happy family. I'm tired of his colleagues, friends, and church members putting him on a pedestal when he is a disgusting, dirty, and selfish old man. They're clueless about him and I'm supposed to keep my mouth shut."

"Oh, my goodness. Are you serious?"

"Yes, I'm serious. My father is a horrible man. I feel so much better now that I've said what he really is. I needed to get it out of my system before I explode. Mother wants me to protect the family and pretend like everything is hunky-dory. What about me? Does anyone care? Has anyone thought about my feelings? Has anyone thought about my mental state of mind? Has anyone thought about what he has done to me? I can't hold it in any longer. I'm going to say it! My father abused me mentally and physically. All he cares about is himself, money, control, status, and power. He treats Mother and me like he owns us. He's a narcissist. He demands Mother to maintain a perfect image that reflects his importance and power. She has no financial independence and she has to get permission from him to purchase anything, no matter how small it is. Before she accepts a job offer, he has to approve it to make sure it's a prestige position to make him look good. Mother never stays on those jobs over three months because they aren't meaningful to her. I don't know how she tolerates him cheating on her. He goes out in public with his women to bars, events, hotels, and vacation for weeks. When mother asks him about his affairs, he tells her to shut up. When she threatens to leave him, he tells her she isn't going anywhere until he is ready for her to go. I asked her to come and live with me, but it will never happen. She is afraid to leave him because of what he is capable of doing to her. I feel so sorry for her.

"He wanted me to be a doctor for status purpose only and he refused to pay my tuition when I left the university to go to culinary school. I made up my mind I was going to finish school whether he helped me or not. I wasn't going to give him the satisfaction of saying I failed. I struggled hard by working part time to finish culinary school and I was finally hired as head chef at a major hotel in Charlotte, North Carolina.

"If Mother didn't live with him, I would never come home. Mother doesn't have anyone to talk to about Father but me. She has cut herself off from her family and friends, and they don't visit anymore. When I miss months coming home, Mother becomes highly sensitive. She cries more easily to general conversations that I thought wouldn't affect her. Because I work most weekends, I can't come home as often as she wants me to. She hung up the phone on me numerous times when I told her I couldn't come home.

"When I came home to visit, Father wouldn't speak to me and he would go in his studying room and slam the door. I didn't care. He did me a favor when he left the room. I came to visit my mother, and she was happy too when he left the room so we could have quality time together without his verbal abuse. Every time I come home, she hugs me and she tells me how much she missed me. Her short, small-framed body makes me feel like her mother sometimes. When she looks up at me with her sad eyes, I want to pick her up and take her home with me. If she comes home with me, I won't have to worry about her anymore.

"This time when I came home, Father needed to go to his medical appointment but he couldn't drive because he wasn't feeling well. He had difficulty breathing, and he was weak and dizzy. Mother had an appointment today for a job interview for a chief operations officer position and her appointment conflicted with his. He didn't want her to miss the interview because he had pulled some strings to get her the interview. After his friend reneged, he reluctantly agreed to me driving him to his appointment. I knew it was going to be a stressful ride and I braced myself for hearing unpleasant words from him.

"Nonstop all the way to the clinic he ranted and raved about the career choice I had made, the disgrace I am to his family, and how ashamed he is of me working in the kitchen. I corrected him and told him I'm a chef. He said, 'You are kitchen help and a second-class citizen. That's who you are! You can dress it up if it makes you feel better.' I thought I could handle him, but I burst into tears. I was exhausted but angry. I didn't have the courage to tell him what I really thought about him. He didn't care I was crying and he didn't care how his words hurt me mentally. He has never told me he loves me and he has never apologized for all the hurt and pain he has caused in my entire life. One day he looked me right in the eye and said, 'I hate you were ever born.' Mother told me he didn't mean it. She said he was angry because I wouldn't change my major. Mother always make excuses for him even though she knows he's wrong."

A nurse passed by us into the examination room and put her pointer finger over her mouth for us to be quiet. The stranger lowered her voice and she walked back to the waiting room and sat down. I followed her and sat beside her. I could tell she felt safe with me because she wasn't afraid to share her painful, vulnerable side. She looked at me and smiled, reaching for me to hold her shaking hands. I held her hand as she continued talking.

"I wanted to tell him I hated him and how disgusting he was. I had thought about killing him so Mother and I would have some peace in our lives. For a second, I forgot I would be in prison for the rest of my life if I killed him. There is no peace in prison. Instead, I contemplated killing myself. I thought about shooting myself in the head, taking sleeping pills, or jumping out of the window of a ten-story building. When I decided to jump out the window, I changed my mind. I had to think about Mother. Taking my life would put Mother into a deeper depression. I couldn't leave her alone with that beast. I'm the only person she trusts and I'm her only child."

I became shocked and saddened as she continued her life story. She had everything that money could buy, but she hadn't had the love and support she'd needed as a child and young adult from her father. Her story continued:

"He taught me there is no proof or evidence that there is a God. He said it was superstitious nonsense and that anyone who believed in God was ignorant. He said only a fool worships someone they can't hear, see, or speak to. He is an atheist and he is proud of it. He values material things and he isn't shy about cutting someone's throat to get ahead."

I was trying to find the right words to say to her without causing more stress and confusion. I wanted to try to help resolve her situation by listening and offering support. How could I tell her to honor her father? How could I tell her to forgive him and to stay close to her parents? Tears were slowly coming down her face. She turned her head away from people as they passed by. It was obvious she didn't want her inner emotions exposed. After silently praying for the right words to say to her, I put my arm around her shoulders. God gave me the right words to encourage her.

"You're beautiful inside and outside, strong, and courageous. I have never met anyone with your determination and willpower. You should be proud of yourself for choosing a career you wanted to do. You have so much love in your heart and so many people are going to be blessed when they meet you. You have already blessed me and I have only known you for a few minutes. Just think about the people who have known you for a long time. I know you have touched their lives in a positive way through your sweet, loving personality and compassion."

She smiled and her eyes began to glow.

"Thank you."

"I want to share a message my parents taught me when I was a teenager that will change your life for the better if you're interested in listening to me."

"Yes, I want to hear what you have to say. I need any help I can get."

Her body language and the desperation in her voice made it apparent she was sincere.

"There is a God and he is with you always if you want him to be. He isn't going to push himself on you. You have to come to him. He's awesome and there isn't anything he can't do. God gave his only son, Jesus, so that we can have eternal life. His love is mighty and he never gives up on us. All you have to do is read the Bible, accept his son, Jesus, as your savior, and pray. He will hear you and speak to you, and you will see yourself as God sees you. You have to go through Jesus to get to God. 'Jesus saith unto him, I am the way, the truth, and the life: no man cometh unto the Father, but by me,' John 14:6. He created you and his purpose for you is to help others see that he exists through your sweet, loving, and kind personality. You will feel like a new person and everything that happened before you gave your life to him will no longer trouble you. You will be reborn! You will pray for the weary and rejoice for the believers."

"Really?"

"Yes, it's true. I'm a living witness."

I reached in my pocketbook and pulled out my lime green pocket Bible. I said, "Even though I had many pocket Bibles, this Bible was special to me. I was depressed because of working for a lousy boss. He micromanaged me, took credit for my hard work, showed favoritism, didn't support me, and focused more on my weaknesses than my strengths. I became sick and couldn't sleep at night from worrying. Walking is my stress relief and I walked every day to calm myself. One day while walking at Burlington

City Park, I found this tiny green Bible on a bench nearby in the same area I always walked. I felt it was meant for me. I was about to explode because I couldn't tolerate my boss's unprofessional behavior any longer. I opened the Bible and smiled when I saw what was inscribed on the first page. The writing said, 'I belong to whoever needs me.' A small, red ribbon bookmarker was placed in the Bible in Psalms. The verse that captured my attention was 'Cast thy burden upon the Lord, and he shall sustain thee: he shall never suffer the righteous to be moved,' Psalm 55:22. God had a mighty sweet way of letting me know he was all I needed for support. I slept like a baby that night. I want you to have this Bible. It will mean a lot to me if you take it, but I won't be offended at all if you don't want it."

"I don't want to take your only Bible."

"I have lots of Bibles at home."

"I would love to have it—I don't own a Bible."

"Well, now you're the proud owner of this little Bible."

"Thank you so much for my Bible and for listening to me. You're a kind person and it was so easy to talk to you. I feel so much better, almost like a new person. I was about to go crazy before I met you."

"You're going to be just fine."

"You think so?"

"I know so."

She kissed me on the cheek and hurried out the waiting room to meet her mother, who was waiting at the exit door. I realized that I didn't know her name and she didn't know mine. As she walked toward her mother, she looked back at me and smiled. I waved goodbye to her and watched her as she left with her mother out the exit door.

"It doesn't matter I don't know her name. We crossed each other's paths for a reason."

My reason for meeting her was to appreciate who I am and to appreciate Daddy's love, protection, and spiritual guidance for his family. I failed to acknowledge his goodness because of being blindsided by people's perspective on living and the things needed in life to accomplish it. I was busy trying to please people instead of pleasing God. The Bible illustrates how we are supposed to live in Heb 13:5: "Let your conversation be without covetousness; and be content with such things as ye have: for he hath said, I will never leave thee, nor forsake thee."

I'm so thankful she redirected my thinking back to God's way. It frightens me knowing that I had come close to losing my faith, which is a major source of meaning in my life. Her purpose for meeting me was to express her inner feelings without being ridiculed and judged. Also, it was time for her to be introduced to God and his son, Jesus Christ, before it was too late. Once she accepts Jesus as her savior, all her hurt and pain will be replaced with healing, forgiveness, and love. Then she will be able to move forward to a healthier, peaceful Christian life. She will find comfort in reading Ps 103:1–6: "Bless the Lord, O my soul: and all that is within me, bless his holy name! Bless the Lord, O my soul, and forget not all his benefits: who forgiveth all thine iniquities; who healeth all thy diseases; who redeemeth thy life from destruction; who crowneth thee with loving kindness and tender mercies; who satisfieth thy mouth with good things; so that thy youth is renewed like the eagle's. The Lord executeth righteousness and judgement for all who are oppressed."

God knew exactly what he was doing when he brought us together to reveal our hidden fears and insecurities that were gradually destroying our souls. He knew before we were born the struggles we would endure and he had a plan waiting for us when he knew we would receive it. He implemented his perfect master plan effectively to encompass all that he has predestined to occur. He is mightier, wiser, and stronger than anyone can ever imagine, and his love for us is powerful.

As soon as she exited out of the door, I felt the need to tell God how I was feeling and thank him for giving me understanding of his will for me. I was anxious to find a private place to pray where I wouldn't be interrupted. A secluded place was necessary, according to the Bible: "But thou, when thou prayest, enter into thy closet, and when thou hast shut thy door, pray to thy Father which is in secret; and thy Father which seeth in secret shall reward thee openly" (Matt 6:6). When a patient came out of the bathroom, I rushed in, locked the door, took a deep breath, sat down on the toilet stool, and began talking to God. God had set me free and the feeling I had was surreal. I felt as though a ton of bricks had been lifted off my shoulders. A lightness entered the bathroom that I spiritually saw and my heart was warm with his mercy and love.

My frustration with life had come because I wasn't satisfied with myself. It prevented me from enjoying an intimate relationship with God and distracted me from appreciating the stability God had provided for me. When I thought about missing God's remarkable miracles all those years, I trembled because I missed a fortune. Joy returned back into my life and I was so thankful. It was the best existence I had ever achieved. Looking good and having things didn't matter anymore. Everything that looks good isn't always good, and wishing to be like someone else is a waste of time. God made everyone different for a reason. For the first time I was completely satisfied and thankful for my own individuality. I felt an overpowering presence of God in the bathroom and a warm sensation traveling throughout my body. What I was feeling was welcome; I was ready for him to use me for his purpose. I wept as I poured my heart out to him.

"I promise you, God, that I will never want to be like anyone else. I was blind, but now I can see. It's not about me. It's about you. Please forgive me for being so selfish."

Out of the blue, I started thinking about Daddy and I began to weep harder. Daddy had done everything a father could possibly do to ensure I was strong enough to live and overcome difficulties without tendencies of being bias or judgmental. He did it by teaching me the Bible and through his actions of Christian faith. I was weeping because I had lived my life the opposite. I know he would have been disappointed at the woman I had become—worrying about what I didn't have and what I should have instead of thanking God for what I have and who I am. After hearing the stranger's story, I recovered lost and forgotten fond memories of my childhood. Without delay, I had a strong yearning for Daddy's hugs, laughter, and stories, and his expressions of love in so many inspiring ways. My daddy, Berkeley Herbert Brown, always made me feel good about myself and would lift me up when I doubted myself. He never harmed me physically or mentally and he protected me from people he knew were negative or dangerous.

"God, thank you for Daddy and all the guidance, teaching, and advice he gave me that money couldn't buy."

I rose from the toilet stool when I heard someone knocking on the door. I unlocked the door and walked out to discover several people waiting to use the restroom. The lady standing first in line gave me a dirty look.

"I was wondering what was taking you so long. I didn't know if you were sick or dead. I was getting ready to get the nurse to unlock the door."

"I'm so sorry. Have a blessed day."

She grunted, hurried into the bathroom, and slammed the door.

There were two other ladies waiting in line too. I smiled at them, but they didn't smile back at me. I decided not to push my luck by apologizing again because of their facial expressions. It was clear they were unpleasant and frustrated. I slowly walked past them and quickly went back into the waiting area to wait for Joann. I was so thankful for my revelation that their negative attitude didn't bother me the least little bit. They had every right to be angry at me. It was a public bathroom and it was selfish of me to use it for a prayer room when there was only one bathroom in the waiting room.

I sat in the waiting room for a while, smiling at every person that came in and out of the clinic. I helped a disabled patient go to the front desk, opened the door for a vendor, and helped a patient with crossword puzzles until she was called back to the nurse's station. In the past, my unhappiness had made me cut myself off from the joy of other people. Being able to make a positive change in the waiting room made me realize I needed people in my life. They helped me find new meaning in my life and acceptance of my own individuality. I saw beauty in all of them and also saw how much they needed love and belonging. Love and belonging are what I needed too. It was amazing how their frowns and sadness became smiles and happiness because of an act of kindness. Taking time and bringing joy to them gave me flashbacks to my younger years with Daddy. He made so many people smile by cheering them up whenever they were in doubt. His friends admired the way he carried himself. He expressed his individuality to them with confidence, and he wasn't afraid to take risk and accept challenges for a better family life. When he failed, he wasn't embarrassed or shameful. He bounced back stronger than before.

"He was one in a million."

I couldn't control the flow of thoughts in my mind about Daddy.

2

Life's Greatest Gift

Daddy taught me that God created everyone equally and that everyone needed each other regardless of background, race, sex, religion, or other differences. Discrimination, racism, and bigotry were words that were never mentioned in our household. When I came along, segregation was unfortunately still alive. Thanks to my parents, I was never in a situation where I felt discriminated against. One day after I had completed my chores to Mama's satisfaction, Daddy rewarded me by taking me to a local restaurant owned by a white family. He had promised to get Mama and me a hotdog "all the way," with mustard, chili, onions, and slaw. Going to a restaurant was a big deal in our household because we had never been to a restaurant before. Mama cooked all our meals and we ate at home. When we arrived at the restaurant, I noticed that white people were entering the front door and African Americans were entering the side door. There was a "color" sign on the side door.

"Daddy, why are we going to the side door and white people are going to the front door?"

"Because we're special."

"I thought everybody is special."

"Everybody is special."

"Well, if everybody is special, why can't we all go to the same door?"

"Because they don't know everyone is special. They haven't figured that out yet."

"Why don't they know it?"

"Somebody didn't tell them."

"You need to tell them."

"Don't worry, they will know soon. It takes time. We can't change people. Jesus has to change them."

Daddy had protected me from racism because he wanted me to love everybody. He was afraid that if I was aware of racism and its history, I would become bitter, angry, and violent. I believed his explanation for the separate doors. That day, I remember holding my head up high and smiling. I thought I was extra special because I had a hotdog and I had entered the restaurant through the side door. I was thankful that God had made me special. That night I prayed for God to help white people figure out they were just as special as I was. Daddy was wise to order the hotdogs to go. If we had eaten in the restaurant, I would have known the reason I couldn't drink out of the same water fountain and use the same bathroom as the white race. When I grew a few years older, I realized race was an issue for many people, both Black and white. I prayed for God to remove the fear of difference from anyone who was struggling with it. Also, I concluded that ignorance, people wanting to be cruel, and the desire to be superior are the roots of racism. It was too late for anyone to change my personality and my views about different races. Daddy had instilled into me the quality of being open-minded and receptive to learning from all races and life situations. Mama was a seamstress and occasionally sewed in our home for customers when they had special requests. Although she made all my clothing, she specialized in custom-made bedspreads, quilts, dust ruffles, Roman curtains, draperies, chair covers, and tablecloths. She took requests from all races in and out of the Piedmont Triad, and Daddy took me with them when he and Mama went to customers' homes to measure windows, beds, chairs, and tables. I remember playing with the white customers' children and having pleasant conversations with them. Because of my parents, I enjoy and love diversity. One of Daddy's favorite scriptures was 1 John 4:7–10: "Beloved, let us love one another: for love is of God, and even one that loveth is born of God, and knoweth God. He that loveth not knoweth not God; for God is love. In this was manifested the love of God toward us, because God sent his only begotten Son into the world, that we might live through him. Herein is love, not that we loved God, but that he loved us, and sent his Son to be the propitiation for our sins."

The waiting room was diverse and almost everyone in the waiting room was kind and helpful to one another. Race, gender, and class wasn't an issue. People laughed and talked together, and their children played games together. They had to have loving and kind parents like Daddy and Mama. After tying a wheelchair patient's shoestrings and opening her water bottle, I walked outside to wait for Joann. I sat on a concrete, gray bench nearby in view of a variety of colorful perennial flowers, flowering dogwood trees, and waterfalls. It was the perfect environment to reminisce in private about the treasures Daddy and Mama had given me—love in so many ways.

"How did you and Mama meet?"

"I met your mama at Mr. Harrison's store on Stoney Creek Road in Caswell County. She and her sisters had walked to the store to buy matches to burn wood in their fireplace. As soon as I got in the store, I saw her standing there. I couldn't take my eyes off of her. When she looked at me with her pretty brown eyes and smiled at me, I couldn't move. She had on a pretty little blue dress and a pair of black flapper shoes. She was dressed like she was going to church. You didn't see women back in those days dressing like your mama. She was so pretty I forgot what I came in the store to buy."

Daddy's facial expressions and the look in his eyes expressed how much he loved Mama. At a young age, I noticed how Daddy showed his love to Mama by thanking God for her when praying and supporting her in what she valued as important to her life. He listened to her, showed her she mattered, complimented her, and protected her. It was wonderful living in an environment full of love, the greatest gift of all from God. I remember Daddy and Mama reading 1 Cor 13:2–8 together to reiterate to me how important love is:

> And though I have the gift of prophecy, and understand all mysteries and all knowledge, and though I have all faith, so that I could remove mountains, but have not love, I am nothing. And though I bestow all my goods to feed the poor, and though I give my body to be burned, but have not love, it profits me nothing. Love suffers long and is kind; love does not envy; love does not parade itself, is not puffed up; does not behave rudely, does not seek its own, is not provoked, thinks no evil; does not rejoice in iniquity, but rejoices in the truth; bears all things, believes all things, hopes all things, endures all things. Love never fails. But whether there are prophecies, they will fail; whether there are tongues, they will cease; whether there is knowledge, it will vanish away.

Daddy smiled and continued telling his love story. "I said, 'What's your name?' She said, 'Willie Elizabeth.' I said, 'You have a pretty name.' She said thank you.

"I said, 'Do you have a boyfriend?' She said yes. I said, 'Why isn't he here with you? If you were my lady, I wouldn't let you walk to the store by yourself.' She said, 'I'm not by myself. My sister is with me and my boyfriend is in the army.' I said, how in the world is he your boyfriend and he isn't here?'

"She turned her head away from me because she knew I was telling the truth. I was smitten and I had to think of a way to get her to like me. Military men thought they could get all the women just because they had on a uniform. Well, I was going to prove them wrong.

"I tapped danced for your mama in the store in front of everybody. I pulled out my harmonica, moved closer to her, and started playing music. She loved it. Her eyes never left my eyes. Everybody in the store was clapping their hands. When your mama asked me to play the harmonica again, I knew she was having a good time. She wouldn't dance with me, but she talked to me and I enjoyed listening to her. She had more than just good looks. She was sweet and smart. She was everything I had wanted in a wife. I was brave unlike in the past. I asked her if I could come and see her. When she said yes, I almost passed out. I didn't waste any time coming to her house and I wasn't afraid to knock on her daddy and mama's door. I did everything I could every time I came to see her to make her happy. Finally, after months of showing her how much I loved her, I asked her to marry me. When she said yes, I was happy. I picked her up and swirled her around the room. I didn't waste any time marrying your sweet mama. I didn't let her get away from me because she is a good woman. I wasn't a fool. She could've married any man she wanted but she didn't look any further when she met me. She knew I loved her and she knew I was a good man. She wasn't a fool either. I knew I didn't have to worry about a thing like some of my friends. They don't know where their wives are half the time. They wouldn't know what a home-cooked meal was if it hit them in the face."

Daddy and I laughed hysterically. He patted me on the head and gave me three sticks of wood to stack on the back porch for the winter. It was the first time I had heard the story of Daddy and Mama meeting. It was a great feeling at eleven years old knowing how much Daddy and Mama loved each other. I was thankful God had given me wonderful parents and I was thankful my parents taught me to pray. I enjoyed praying to God every night about different things, and I loved the prayers I learned in church the best because I remembered them. That night and every night after Daddy's story about meeting Mama, I added Mama and Daddy into my prayers. A memorized prayer just didn't seem right to me anymore. The prayers I said that night and every night afterward were meaningful to me because they came from my heart. I felt closer to God.

"God bless Daddy and God bless Mama. They're good to me and they do a lot for me. Daddy works hard for us to have a house, he buys food for us to eat, and he reads the Bible. God, he loves us very much. Mama cooks, cleans, washes our clothes, and irons. She reads the Bible and she loves us very much too. She kisses me at night when I go to bed and she kisses me when I wake up. She hugs me every time she sees me. God please bless everyone and keep them safe. Thank you, God, for everything. Amen."

3

Daddy's Good Book

Daddy and Mama were raised in Caswell, North Carolina. Caswell was formed from a northern portion of Orange County in 1777. The county was named after Richard Caswell, governor of North Carolina. It was in Caswell County that the Slade family discovered the process of curing tobacco leaves that revolutionized the tobacco industry, bringing wealth to many farmers, including African Americans.[1]

My grandparents on both sides of my family were fortunate to inherit many acres of land where they grew tobacco and vegetables. They also raised pigs, cows, and chickens to eat and sell at meat markets. The vegetables were frozen and canned for their families, and also sold to local farmers markets throughout the county. Mama and Daddy inherited farming skills, but they didn't grow tobacco or raise animals for income. Mama was a homemaker and a professional seamstress. Daddy was a truck driver and eventually worked in the school system. After Daddy married Mama, they lived in Caswell County for a few years and eventually moved to Burlington, North Carolina, where they resided until they died.

Burlington is a city in Alamance County. Alamance County was created when Orange County was portioned out in 1849, and in the 1850s there was a need for a railroad in North Carolina. The citizens of Alamance County needed land where they could build, repair, and do maintenance on the track. Land was purchased by citizens who could afford it, and on January 29, 1856, the last spikes of the North Carolina Railroad were driven successfully. Soon after it opened, citizens realized they needed repair shops to meet demands and work efficiently. By 1859, construction of the shops began. A church, bank, and hotel were up and running. The town was called Company Shops. When the shops were completed, the village had grown to twenty-seven buildings. Thirty-nine white men, twenty Negro slaves, and two free Negroes were employed at the shops. Soon they were selling, but the sales were slow until after the Civil War. By 1864, the population of Company Shops was about three hundred people. After twenty-five years of operations, the shops of most of the railroad facilities closed. Since the railroad closed, the citizens of Company Shops decided a new name was needed for their city. Company Shops was renamed "Burlington" on February 14, 1864. The city of Burlington was incorporated and a charter was issued by the state legislature. The city continued to grow and in 1908, E. M. Holt built the first cotton mill in Burlington. As time passed, Alamance County operated thirty cotton mills and ten to fifteen yarn-manufacturing plants, employing fifteen thousand people. Burlington became a prosperous little city with churches, schools, newspapers, and telegraph and telephone lines.[2]

It is now known for upscale shopping centers, retail stores, and fine dining restaurants specializing in American, Chinese, Japanese, Italian, Mexican, Indian, and Greek dishes. The citizens of Burlington were like family and most of them were always there for each other in time of need. If they had a dime, you had five cents and if they had a dozen of eggs, you had six eggs. The women in the neighborhood took care of each other's children when both parents were working and didn't have a sitter. They never charged to keep them and they were never afraid to hug them to express their love. Children respected the adults and if they misbehaved the neighbors corrected them without repercussions. The men used their carpentry skills to help the neighbors build, repair, renovate, and paint each other's homes, barns, and storage sheds when needed. During the summers, the residents of Burlington had barbecue, Brunswick stew, fish fry, pie, cake, and chitterling sales to raise money for churches, community events, and neighborhood projects. Daddy and Mama supported each fundraiser by bringing fruits and vegetables to help raise money. My favorite place in Burlington was in the rural areas on the outskirts of town. We had fruit trees, strawberries, muscadine grape bushes, and a little garden. I loved picking the tomatoes off the vine and eating them for a snack. I could yell, scream, and turn up the volume on the television without the neighbors complaining because they couldn't hear us. The two acres of property we lived on and the Leyland cypress trees gave us privacy and quality time together without disturbing our neighbors.

Daddy was a tall, strong, muscular, handsome African American man, and he had big strong hands. His hands could hold just about anything, including me. I was amazed as a child at how he could lift and move heavy equipment effortlessly and how he could build anything. In his toolbox, he always had a club, sledge, and claw hammer. He would include me in all the house projects he did for Mama. I loved hammering a nail into a wooden object even though I had a difficult time getting the nail completely into the wood. I would get tickled at him when he tried to hold my unsteady hand in the right position to hit the head of the nail.

"You can do a better job if you stop laughing."

"Okay Daddy."

I was unsuccessful, but I felt good about trying because of Daddy's encouraging words. Failure wasn't a negative feeling when I was working with Daddy.

"Don't worry about it, baby. Keep nailing and your strength will come. The more you do it, the better you will get. One day you're going to be strong enough to nail down a house."

He was rich in heart and it frustrated him when he couldn't earn enough money to buy what we wanted. We had what we needed. Now I realize he gave me so much that the material things don't matter. He instilled in me courage, strength, determination, loyalty, honesty, dedication, kindness, and compassion for others. Mama assisted Daddy in making sure my personality stayed intact without neglecting my physical and emotional needs. They were a team with the same goals for their daughter.

"It is true a child will live what they learn."

Daddy provided for his family the best he could with no education, trade, or skills. I never saw Daddy drink alcoholic beverages or smoke. He was clearheaded and stayed away from confusion and gossip. He never stayed out late at night or hung out with a crowd. Daddy loved Mama dearly. He would tell me he had the prettiest woman in town and I believed he was sincere. Mama was strikingly beautiful and classy. She had long, thick black hair, appealing lips, a gorgeous figure, and shapely legs. Her brown skin was like velvet, and lipstick was the only makeup she used. She walked with confidence and she was intellectually challenging. When Mama looked at Daddy with her beautiful, charming eyes, Daddy was like a little boy craving a lollipop. Every Sunday, I saw Daddy staring at Mama as she put on her stylish dress and her high-heel patent shoes. He couldn't take his eyes off of her. If he saw me looking at him, he would quickly turn his head in another direction from Mama. He wanted to maintain his image as a father and he didn't want me to lose the respect I had for him. Little did he know I loved the way he looked at Mama and I respected him even more because he still had desire for her.

Daddy was well-liked in the community because he listened to people. He was plentiful with favors, advised people and kept an eye on them, and rescued anyone that needed him.

"Daddy, you're nice to everyone you meet."

"God wants us to love each other as brothers and sisters. It's hard to do sometimes, but with the help of God you can do it. You will feel so much better being nice instead of being mean to people."

"I'm not mean to nobody."

"You stay that way and you'll be blessed."

Even though I believed everything Daddy said, he always referred to the Bible when teaching right from wrong: "Let brotherly love continue. Be not forgetful to entertain strangers: for thereby some have entertained angels unawares" (Heb 13:1–2).

Daddy went to church, had faith and trusted in God, taught me to be a "good girl," and used the Bible as a guide for parenting. He was a believer in knowledge and was always enthusiastic about answering any questions I had, regardless of how annoying they were. The question and answer sessions we had together gave me courage and freedom to express my opinions with a positive mindset. He always clarified any questions or concerns in a gentle and caring way, which resulted in a healthy-attachment relationship and bond between the two of us. One early morning I woke up to use the bathroom. I saw Daddy out on the screened-in porch reading his King James Bible. When I was a teenager, I didn't understand why it was so important for him to read the Bible when he should be resting. Now, I realize he needed God to guide him in the right direction, and he had faith and trust in him. After pondering for a few minutes, I went out on the porch to see what he was reading.

"Good morning, sunshine. What are you doing up so early?"

"Good morning, Daddy. I had to use the bathroom."

"You shouldn't drink too much tea before going to bed. I bet you will listen next time."

I chuckled and began asking questions.

"Daddy, what are you reading?"

"I'm reading a scripture in the good book."

"Why are you reading a scripture?"

"It makes me feel better."

"Why does it make you feel better?"

"It reminds me that no matter what I'm going through, God loves me. He will never let you down and he won't tell a lie on you or hurt you. He will protect us and help us. You don't have to worry about a thing if you count on God."

"What does 'count on God' mean?"

"It means God will always be in your life even when you don't think he's there. He will never change, and his love will never go away no matter what you do or say."

"Even if I don't do my chores or homework?"

"That's right."

"He really loves us a lot."

"The best love in the world."

"Wow! I'm glad he loves me too."

"And he wants us to love him and if you love him, you will love everyone."

"Do you love God?"

"I love him more than life."

"I love him too."

"That is good. I was getting ready to read the good book alone but I think I would rather read it with you. Do you want me to read it to you?"

"Yes Daddy, read it to me."

I leaned on Daddy's left shoulder while he read the Bible to me. At my early age, I didn't know he was reading 1 John 4:1–6, 11–21.

> Beloved, believe not every spirit, but try the spirits whether they are of God: because many false prophets are gone out into the world. Hereby know ye the Spirit of God: Every spirit that confesseth that Jesus Christ is come in the flesh is of God: And every spirit that confesseth not that Jesus Christ is come in the flesh is not of God: and this is that spirit of antichrist, whereof ye have heard that it should come; and even now already is it in the world. Ye are of God, little children, and have overcome them: because greater is he that is in you, than he that is in the world. They are of the world: therefore speak they of the world, and the world heareth them. We are of God: he that knoweth God heareth us; he that

is not of God heareth not us. Hereby know we the spirit of truth, and the spirit of error . . . Beloved, if God so loved us, we ought also to love one another. No man hath seen God at any time. If we love one another, God dwelleth in us, and his love is perfected in us. Hereby know we that we dwell in him, and he in us, because he hath given us of his Spirit. And we have seen and do testify that the Father sent the Son to be the Saviour of the world. Whosoever shall confess that Jesus is the Son of God, God dwelleth in him, and he in God. And we have known and believed the love that God hath to us. God is love; and he that dwelleth in love dwelleth in God, and God in him. Herein is our love made perfect, that we may have boldness in the day of judgment: because as he is, so are we in this world. There is no fear in love; but perfect love casteth out fear: because fear hath torment. He that feareth is not made perfect in love. We love him, because he first loved us. If a man say, I love God, and hateth his brother, he is a liar: for he that loveth not his brother whom he hath seen, how can he love God whom he hath not seen? And this commandment have we from him, That he who loveth God love his brother also.

"What is 'Antichrist?'"

"It's a person that is an enemy of God trying to win all of God's people by telling them untruths about him. The Antichrist doesn't believe in anything right but everything wrong. The Antichrist is nothing but a wicked and evil beast. That's why it's important to read and live by the good book. Reading the good book will answer all your questions and keep you from sinning. You won't have to worry about the Antichrist because God will protect you."

I remember him sitting me on his lap and explaining how God loved us so much that he gave his only son, Jesus, so that we could have everlasting life.

"Daddy, did God cry when they nailed Jesus to the cross?"

"I don't know. I'm sure he was sad, but it was in God's plan for Jesus to die so we can live in heaven forever. But we can't live forever in heaven if we don't believe in God. We have to ask God to forgive us of our sins too."

"I will ask him tonight when I say my prayers."

"Good. God is going to be so happy."

I yawned and wiped my eyes to keep me from falling asleep. I was tired from asking questions and I didn't understand most of Daddy's answers. Daddy kissed me on the cheek and walked me back to my bedroom. He waited until I said my prayer and got into bed before leaving the room.

I was overwhelmed with joy that I'd had quality time with him alone. I was exhausted that night and slept like a baby. I was definitely a daddy's girl.

4

Coming Home Late

Daddy didn't have any problems correcting me when I didn't follow his rules. Daddy had rules for everything, including rules for school. He was adamant about me coming straight home after school. One of the school rules was that when school was over, I couldn't hang out with my classmates at a nearby store where arguments and fights had occurred in the past. After and before school, I couldn't stop at anyone's house or bring them to our home. I had chores and homework that had to be done, and friends couldn't visit until the end of the school week, and they could only come if my tasks were completed. Friends were only allowed to come and visit if they met Daddy's criteria. If he didn't see them in church with their parents, he was skeptical about their Christian faith and their values. I could only play with children and family members on the weekend that were in our church circle or other churches. One day before school ended, my teacher asked me and my classmate, Rebecca, if we could stay after school to help her in the cafeteria. She wanted us to help her prepare for the senior baccalaureate ceremony that was going to be held the next day at Jordan Sellars High School. She needed help making a variety of miniature sandwiches and filling decorative trays with peanuts, cheese straws, buttered mints, and cookies. It was an honor and a privilege to be asked to help with the senior commencement activities. I didn't think it through and made an impulsive decision. I said yes without thinking about the consequences. This was an opportunity of a lifetime and I wasn't going to miss it. Even though Mama had told me many times that God doesn't answer selfish prayers, I prayed anyway.

"Dear God, don't let Daddy be mad at me for staying after school. I'm staying to help my teacher. She can't do it by herself. He shouldn't be mad at me because Mrs. Summers goes to our church and she comes to Mama's prayer meetings every Wednesday night. If he gets mad at me, please tell him to give me a second chance. Amen."

I was very serious and focused on making a good impression on my teacher, which would result in a successful school year. I knew Mrs. Summers would appreciate my efforts as well as my attitude. Color coordinating and arranging food were skills I had acquired from church functions and from prayer meetings at home. Without being told, Rebecca followed suit. We styled the food to look elegant and appetizing with a touch of sophistication. After ransacking every storage closet in the building, I found beautiful off-white lace tablecloths for the tables. I borrowed flowers from some of the teacher's classrooms and arranged them on the table for centerpieces. Everything was on the table except for the miniature sandwiches. We put them in the refrigerator for the next day to go on the table in the areas we had designated. I placed plates at the beginning of the table and silverware and napkins at the end of the table. The punch bowls and glasses were on two small tables away from the entrance to help prevent people from crowding around the food and drink. When teachers passed by, they stopped to admire the beautiful tables and to thank us for a job well done. After we tightly covered the food with plastic wrap, placed the sandwiches in the refrigerator, and cleaned up, Rebecca and I sat down to rest. Mrs. Summers smiled as she walked down the tables in admiration. She was so proud of us.

"I knew you would do a good job! Wow! Look at these trays. The way you arranged the food makes it look so delicious. My little friends, you really did it! This is amazing! These tables are so neat and beautifully arranged. There isn't one crumb on the table. Oh my goodness! Thank you so much."

She gave each of us a big brown paper bag filled with miniature sandwiches, cheese straws, peanuts, buttered mints, and five dollars. It was the most money I had ever had at one time!

Rebecca and I hugged each other and waved goodbye as we headed home in opposite directions. There was something special about Rebecca's personality. She was kind, patient, helpful, peaceful, and focused—all the traits I needed in a friend.

Walking home alone wasn't frightening; it was relaxing. It gave me time to plan how I was going to spend my money.

"I'm going to give Daddy and Mama a dollar apiece, buy some ribbons for my hair, and get an ice-cream cone. Two dollars for Daddy and Mama, twenty-five cents plus tax for the jack rock game, and ten cents for the ice-cream cone. I will have two dollars and sixty-some cents left to put in my piggy bank. Oh my goodness! I have a lot of money!"

Walking home was an adventure and I noticed things I had never noticed before. Maybe it was because I was happy about my earnings and surpassing Mrs. Summer's expectations. The beautiful homes along the way were in good condition. It was evident the homeowners took pride in their homes and worked hard to keep their homes in tip-top shape. People were out in their yards mowing their lawns, watering and planting flowers, and washing their cars. Everyone was friendly and waved at me as I passed by their houses. Although traffic was slow on the road, drivers were very respectful by slowing down to prevent from hitting me. That day walking home was refreshing and soothing. When I had almost reached home, I saw Daddy walking up the hill toward me. My stomach was in knots and I couldn't take another step. I wanted to run but I knew I would get a spanking. He stood in front of me and looked me in the eyes. I started crying.

"I'm not going to say anything to you right now because I'm mad. I thought something had happened to you. You get home right now, and we will talk about this later."

"I was helping Mrs. Summers. She paid me five dollars. I'm going to give you and Mama a dollar."

"That is your money. You earned it. The money you earned is not the problem. As I just said, we will talk about it when I'm ready to talk."

I didn't say another word. When I arrived home, I put the snack bag on the table and went to my bedroom without eating dinner. Mama came in my bedroom and sat on the bed next to me.

"Edna, you need to come to the table and eat."

"I'm not hungry. I ate before I left school."

Mama kissed me on the cheek and left my room to give me privacy. I needed time alone to pray.

"Dear God, help me. Daddy is mad at me and he won't talk to me. Please tell him to talk to me."

Daddy talked to me the next morning during breakfast.

"I don't care who the person is—you don't stay after school without me or your mama knowing where you are. You know why? Because we love you and we don't want anything to happen to you. What you did was good, but I can't excuse the fact that you did it without asking us. Don't you ever do this again. Do you understand what I just said to you?"

"Yes Daddy, I understand. I promise I won't do it again."

"I believe you. Now let's get off this subject. You have one week left of school and then you will be out for the summer. You have made good grades all year long and we're proud of you."

"Thank you."

That evening, I finally got the courage to ask Mama and Daddy if they wanted to share the food I had prepared for the senior baccalaureate. Without hesitation, they accepted my offer with enthusiasm. Mama's favorite snack was the sandwiches and Daddy's favorite snacks were the cheese straws and buttered mints. They had a friendly debate at the table about the ingredients used to make them and Mama joked about Daddy's inexperience in cooking. Of course, Mama won the debate because Daddy knew nothing about cooking. The laughter at the table was good for my soul and I was thankful that Daddy and Mama had forgotten about my bad behavior. Mama was so pleased with the way I had cut and arranged the sandwiches that she asked me to make sandwiches for her prayer meetings. Prayer meetings became more enjoyable because I helped Mama make homemade chicken salad, pimento cheese, and beef sandwiches with gravy. Her guests complimented me on how beautiful the sandwiches were arranged on the platters.

Daddy and Mama didn't mention the incident again and neither did I. I never stayed after school again and I never told my friends what happened that day. I was too embarrassed to tell anyone that I disobeyed my parents.

5

A Wholesome Tongue

Even though Daddy scolded me when I didn't respect his rules, advice, and teachings, he rewarded me when I was good. He was strict, and his goal for me was that I be the best I could be without losing the faith, dignity, pride, morals, and values that he and Mama had taught me. He always built me up and he never put me down. He made me feel like I could do anything I wanted to do. He wouldn't take anything from anyone but he would give no matter how little he had. He never tried to compete with our neighbors and friends and he didn't want the same things they wanted: status, money, power, and material things. He was a man of substance and it was evident that he didn't feel less important than anyone. You could tell this by his walk, talk, and self-confidence. His passions were the welfare of his family and having a safe, loving, and healthy home through hard work and honesty. He was proud, God-fearing, and hardworking, and he encouraged people when they were down. I never heard him talk negatively about anyone, but I did hear him praise his neighbors and friends all the time.

One early Saturday morning, Daddy took me with him to a car parts junkyard in Caswell County to purchase a used, wide, white wall tire to match the other tires on his 1953 Ford Customline car. It felt like we had walked an hour before he found the tire he was looking for. I was tired and my aching legs could barely keep up with his pace. When he spotted a white wall tire lying against the fence, he came to a complete stop. He looked at the size of the tire and smiled.

"Well, I'll be John Brown! This tire looks brand new and it's the exact size I'm looking for."

He patted me on the head.

"After I pay for the tire, we can head back home."

"Okay."

He was happy, I was happy, and my legs were happy the walk was over. Daddy picked up the tire effortlessly and we walked back to the unpainted, lopsided shack to pay for it. The shack was dirty and had oil spots all over the floor. There was no place for me to sit while Daddy waited in line because automobile parts were all over the place. The men greeted Daddy and some of them shook his hands. It was obvious they all knew each other. One of the men started talking about a family who needed food, clothing, and money. Everyone joined in the conversation except for Daddy. One man was bad-mouthing the Mayfield family and the other men chimed in with their negative opinions. Daddy listened but didn't say one word about the situation. After paying for the tire, Daddy and I quickly left the shack. When we got in the car and drove off, Daddy made a serious comment to me.

"I don't know what is wrong with these so-called Christians who go to church every Sunday. Lord have mercy! Edna, don't never speak badly of people and pray for the ones who do. The good book says to 'treat others the way you want them to treat you,' Matthew 7:12. The good book says, 'Let no corrupt communication proceed out of your mouth, but that which is good to the use of edifying, that it may minister grace unto the hearers' (Eph 4:29). You'll never go through life without having some hard times and you're going to need somebody to help or listen to you before you leave this world. We're going to pray for God to let good words come out of their mouths and to keep their mouths shut if they can't.

When we arrived home, Daddy and Mama went to their bedroom to have a private discussion. Mama and Daddy came out of the bedroom and went right to the kitchen. Mama took out a few bags from the kitchen closet and sat them on the kitchen table. Mama packed the bags with half a bag of flour, a half gallon of milk, six eggs, a half jar of molasses, half a pound of butter, half a pound of cheese, six cans of beef with gravy, half a slab of bacon, half a pound of sausage, and a gallon of hominy, and also added a bushel of fruits and vegetables from the garden. I couldn't believe she had packed half of everything we had to eat. Daddy took all the bags and the bushel of fruits and vegetables out to the car. I didn't know where we were going and I didn't ask any questions. I knew for sure they were helping someone in need because they were creatures of habit. They would give their last dime to help someone in hardship. Daddy had driven about thirty minutes before we turned off on a long, bumpy dirt road. The white, wood-framed house was sitting in the middle of wild trees and beautiful flowers in the front yard, which didn't have grass. Because I had seen a bear in the woods, I wasn't too happy when Daddy told me to stay in the car. A woman and man came out of the house and stood on their porch. They waved at Mama and Daddy and signaled for them to come into their home. Mama and Daddy got out of the car, took the bags and the bushel of fruits and vegetables, and sat them down on the porch. Daddy shook the man's hand and Mama gave the woman a hug. Daddy and the man took the food into the house, laughing and talking as they entered. They stayed in their friends' home for a long time and I became frustrated waiting for my parents to return to the car. Finally, I fell asleep and didn't wake up until I heard Daddy slam the door shut. The only conversation Daddy and Mama had on the way home was about the weather, church, and God. They didn't mention one word about the name of the family or about their situation. It was easy for me to figure out that the family they were helping was the Mayfield family. Daddy and Mama were so kind to help out their friends even though they didn't have an abundance to give. They gave sincerely from their hearts without wanting praise or any kind of recognition. I learned that day that if I have anything to give and see someone in need, I should give—no matter how big or small. Daddy and Mama did exactly what 1 John 3:17–18 says: "But whoso hath this world's good, and seeth his brother have need, and shutteth up his bowels of compassion from him, how dwelleth the love of God in him? My little children, let us not love in word, neither in tongue; but in deed and in truth."

Talking negatively about someone was one of Daddy's pet peeves. That night, Daddy's tiredness didn't prevent him from reading the Bible to corroborate his Christian conviction: "A soft answer turneth away wrath: but grievous words stir up anger. The tongue of the wise useth knowledge aright: but the mouth of fools poureth out foolishness. The eyes of the Lord are in every place, beholding the evil and the good. A wholesome tongue is a tree of life: but perverseness therein is a breach in the spirit" (Prov 15:1–4). "Set a watch, O Lord, before my mouth; keep the door of my lips" (Ps 141:3). Throughout my life, I have never participated in talking negatively about someone in need, but I have struggled with looking for the good in people instead of the bad. If I was mistreated, I told the world about it. As I grew older and experienced life's challenges, I realized the world can't help the situation. Only God can. I finally got it right.

6

Warm Socks

Cutting and bringing in wood for our huge fireplace was a chore Daddy enjoyed doing. He cut wood the same size every time without using a tape measure. After cutting the wood with an axe, he arranged it neatly in a pile for easy pickup. The fresh-cut wood gave off a pungent smell and the wood chips were saved for the summer. Mama used the wood chips to cook meats and vegetables in an open fire in the backyard. A firepit was dug in the ground to contain the fire for safety. It was the best food ever! Daddy wouldn't allow his neighbors or Mama to help him. He took pride in woodcutting and he didn't want any of his neighbors taking credit for his work. When Mama tried to help, he would tell her to stay inside where it was warm, and he told the neighbors he didn't need any help. He always thanked them for wanting to help. I helped him without asking because we had an agreement that I could help him anytime I wanted to. After the completion of each job, he would reward me with a dime, which was the amount needed to buy an ice-cream cone from the community ice-cream truck. He had instilled in me the idea that working was imperative for me to be independent. After taking the last piece of wood to the porch, I hurried to the ice-cream-truck stop before the driver took off. Exhausted, I stopped running and gave a sigh of relief when I saw him parked and filling up wafer cones with ice cream for the children. It was so much fun gathering around the ice-cream truck with my long-time neighborhood friends. We licked each other's ice-cream cones to get a taste of different flavors, and we didn't care about getting germs or a cold from each other. We ate our ice-cream cones, talked, laughed, skipped, and played hopscotch with each other before our curfew was over.

Daddy expressed his love for me in special, sweet, and loving ways. During the school term, he sharpened all my pencils for school, wrote my name on my lunch bag, wiped my runny nose before leaving for school, buttoned up my coat in the winter, and warmed my socks every cold morning to keep my feet warm as long as possible. He wouldn't put cold socks on my feet because he felt I would be at a greater risk of getting a "bad cold." It was so much fun picking out my favorite socks and bringing them to Daddy to warm. Most of my socks were white, with a few blues, pinks, blacks, and browns. He didn't care what color I chose as long as there were no holes in them. Mama ironed everything, including my socks, and she made sure clean socks were plentiful. She had neatly folded them together in four dresser drawers to prevent me from selecting mismatched socks. Daddy was always in the same area of the house near the woodstove and in the same chair waiting for me to bring them. It was the greatest time of my life and the most cherished memory I had with Daddy as a child. Seeing Daddy warming my socks on the woodstove in the kitchen grabbed my attention. He didn't take his eyes off the socks while they were warming. In my opinion, God was the only person smarter than him. He could do anything! Daddy sat me on his lap and massaged my feet before warming my socks. Even though he never told me, he massaged them to release my anxiety about going to school. Later in life, I realized that massaging my feet helped improve my circulation and blood flow for a relaxing walk to school. I enjoyed walking every day regardless of the weather.

Before Daddy put my socks on my feet, he would test them by placing them on the side of his face to make sure they weren't over- or underheated. The socks were never too hot or too cold. The temperature of the socks was always just right. The warm socks made me feel special, significant, and loved, and I appreciated having a daddy who carved time out from his busy schedule to spend sacred time with me. I remember asking him every question I could think of to prolong my stay on his lap.

"Do you like putting warm socks on my feet?"

"Yes, I do."

"Why do you like it?"

"Because it's a treat for my sweet little girl."

"And because you love me."

"That's right."

"They feel so good on my feet, Daddy."

"There's nothing like warm socks in the wintertime. Warm socks can keep you from getting a cold and it warms your spirit."

"Did your daddy put warm socks on your feet?"

"No, he didn't, but he made us a bed from a tree to sleep in."

"Wow! Can you make a bed?"

"I'm afraid I'm not that good at making beds."

"It's okay, Daddy. I love the bed you bought me."

"I'm glad you love it."

"It's story time, Daddy."

While sitting on Daddy's lap, he entertained me with short stories. Story time was exciting as long as it had a happy ending. His stories were mysteries and he made them up on the spur of the moment. His deep voice made his stories more interesting, and the suspense of his stories made me more eager to know the end.

"Once upon a time on a dead-end street in a little pink house lived a little girl named Lula. One summer she never came out of her house, but she would look out her window and watch people pass by. There was a stranger standing at the window with her who had a colorful scarf wrapped around her head. For the first time that summer, there was a 'No Trespassing' sign displayed on the edge of their property line. Every now and then her daddy, John, would leave the house for a short while and come back with grocery bags. Her mama, Ida, wasn't seen watering or planting beautiful flowers like she had done every summer. Passersby began to gossip about what they thought was going on and spread stories throughout the town. Soon the policemen were knocking at their door, demanding to come in to make sure everything was alright. They found out quickly what was going on. The stranger, Helen, was a midwife who had delivered Lula's baby sister, Ella. Lula stayed in the house because she didn't want to leave her mama's side because she was bedridden and needed one-on-one care. John felt it was necessary to display the 'No Trespassing' sign to give Ida proper rest, and he bought the food to cook for the family. The policemen were frustrated and embarrassed. They apologized for intruding and they promised never to listen to anyone else unless they had facts. They were excited to know their trip wasn't wasted. They sat down at the dinner table with the family and enjoyed the delicious food John had cooked."

"What a good story, Daddy!"

"Yep. It shows you how your tongue can get you in trouble. Never tell what you think. Tell what you know and use your tongue to tell good things about people."

There's nothing like having warm socks on your feet when listening to a good story. My friends bragged and shared many stories about their parents: trips they took, gifts and allowances they received, famous people they met, and elaborate restaurants they ate in. I wasn't jealous because not one of my friends had the privilege of their parents warming their socks on a woodstove and sitting them on their laps to put their socks on. It was the greatest gift I had ever received from Daddy. Warming my socks resulted in a beautiful and deep lifetime bond between Daddy and me.

7

One Side of a Story

Daddy taught me to never listen to one side of a story and to forgive because it would give me peace of mind. He said holding a grudge would make your body sick and your mind "crazy." I remember one evening after school my heart was broken because I was told a friend had lied on me. I was crying so hard I could barely see to get home and I didn't care if I lived or died. I promised myself I would punch him in the face if I saw him the next day at school. I struggled to get home because I was heartbroken and afraid people were talking about me. I ran into the house, slammed the front door, and almost knocked Mama over trying to get to my bedroom. Daddy was sitting in the rocking chair reading a magazine and eating popcorn. Mama looked over at Daddy, waiting for him to respond.

"Slow down. What is wrong with you?"

"Michael told Earnestine a story on me."

"What did he say about you?"

"He said he kissed me and he didn't. I would never let him put his lips on me."

"Did you talk to Michael about it?"

"No. I don't ever want to see him again."

"How could you be mad at him when you're not sure if he said it?"

"He said it. Earnestine wouldn't tell me a story."

"Maybe she is telling the truth, or she could be confused. Earnestine is human just like everybody else, and humans make mistakes. Don't you think it's fair to give him a chance to explain?"

"I don't know."

"Michael seems like a pretty nice fellow. He doesn't look or act like he would hurt anyone intentionally. Of course, I could be wrong too. That's why you need to talk to him."

"What if he says he did say it?"

"You pray and forgive him. If he says he didn't say it, pray for Helen and forgive her."

Mama chimed in.

"What would God do?"

It was difficult to do, but I calmed down and called Michael. Daddy and Mama stood beside me for support during the entire conversation. I was amazed when Michael told me that Helen had approached him inquiring about our friendship. She asked him if he liked me, if he had kissed me, and if I was his girlfriend. He said he didn't answer her because he didn't know why she was asking him those silly questions. When I confronted Earnestine with Michael's side of the story, she changed her story. She said she thought I had kissed Michael because he didn't answer her. Daddy was right as usual. At a young age I learned there is more than one side to a story.

The experience of Michael and Earnestine taught me to be fair to the staff I managed in my adult life. It is necessary to have a open door policy for employees to voice their concerns outside their own chain of command without worry. But to make a management decision about an employee based on what a staff member said instead of facts is unfair to the employee. Also, if a decision is made based on falsehood, legal actions may be warranted against the organization resulting in fines, probation, cash settlements, rehiring, back pay, and the loss of the organization's integrity. Legal actions bring their own amount of stress, and the organization depended on me to prevent this. I was determined to reduce stress in the workplace by using strategies and approaches that would boost employee morale. Being stress-free and having peace of mind was essential for the staff in the workplace. It improved their work performance. I secretly named my management style the 'Michael and Earnestine Approach.' One way my approach was used was to prevent a simple disagreement or concern from becoming major. It was much easier for me to nip a disagreement or concern in the bud before it grew out of hand and became too big for me to resolve on my own. My motto was "No employees should feel they're treated unfairly and unappreciated." My open door policy was for supervisors and the employees they managed. My goals were to make them feel valued by recognizing how their skills and abilities empowered others and by using team building and incentives. Without hesitation, all the staff wanted to address their concerns or problems. They trusted me. It was a success! After listening to all sides of the staff members' stories, 100 percent of their stories changed when I brought them in conference together to resolve the issue in a caring way. Not one employee or supervisor left our clinic review meeting dissatisfied. They left the meeting with an appreciation and respect for each other's responsibilities. Their work relationship grew into trust, understanding, and empathy toward each other. They became a strong team and the goals and mission of the organization were accomplished. Mistakes weren't frowned on but used as an opportunity to improve customer and employee satisfaction. Those employees became outstanding in their jobs because of the care, training, coaching, communication, and counseling they received from their directors, managers, supervisors, and peers. They advanced to higher positions in the workplace and higher education.

My parents also taught me to take ownership of my behavior and not blame others. Daddy and Mama's motto was "Make sure you're not the problem before you blame someone else." They listened to all sides of a story to get a bigger picture of an issue, and they addressed the issue with me and the other children together. I was never afraid to work out a situation with my friends because I knew Daddy and Mama was going to bring peace between us. They didn't treat me differently because I was their daughter. Everyone was treated the same. We all had a chance to explain our actions, even though our stories changed when we were face-to-face. Daddy and Mama didn't comment on our story changing but delivered their message to us with empathy. They stressed the importance of playing fair. No one left the house mad. The next day we played together and made sure everyone had a turn playing hopscotch, jack rocks, and marble games.

8

Aunt Katie's Butter Cookies

Daddy depended on me to do "big chores." I would ride with him to Big Bear Supermarket to buy food for the family. He gave me the responsibility of getting the items on the grocery list and selecting a dessert to surprise Mama. He would cross out items as I placed them in the grocery cart and walk in front of me to move an item sitting high on a shelf to a lower shelf for me to reach. He would put the big items in the basket because I wasn't strong enough to lift them and push the cart when it became difficult for me to roll it around the store. Before we got to the cash register, he would give me cash to pay for the groceries. I don't know how he knew how much money to give me, but he always gave me enough and I always got change back. Daddy gave me the change because I did a great job. I felt important and valued and appreciated by my family.

The ride in Daddy's truck was so much fun. He sat me in his lap to teach me how to change gears. He would communicate to me if I was changing gears correctly or if I needed improvement. I remember the advice he gave me; I became an expert in changing gears without scraping them. He said I was so good I was ready for the next step. Gradually he taught me how to guide the steering wheel, and after a few trips to the grocery store, I was steering with no assistance. I did everything except use the gas and brake pedals because I was too short to reach them. I was so excited when my allowance was raised from ten cents to twenty-five cents.

Daddy was an unknown artist and it was a hobby he took pride in. He could draw anything and he did it effortlessly. His Mother Nature drawings were breathtaking and I was proud that Daddy had such an amazing talent. When he finished a drawing, I would hug him and tell him how much I loved his pictures. I remember one day he had drawings rolled up with a rubber band around them. He was excited that a store manager wanted to buy his pictures and I was excited that his work was acknowledged. When he opened his truck door on the passenger's side, I knew it was permission for me to go with him to deliver his drawings. I jumped in the truck and didn't ask any questions. I felt privileged that I was allowed to go. When we arrived downtown at a clothing store, a tall, white, distinguished man walked up to the truck. Daddy unrolled his drawings on the hood of his truck and began talking to the man. I couldn't hear what they were saying, but I knew instantly that the man was pleased with the drawings. He smiled, reached into his pocket, and gave Daddy some bills. I never knew how much money the man paid him because Daddy never discussed his personal and financial business to me. What was most important to me was that his artwork was good enough to sell. I never saw him sell another piece of artwork, but I did see him give away many drawings. I realized that drawing was his hobby and that it was therapeutic, especially when he had a stressful day at work. The screened-in back porch was his place to draw and meditate.

Daddy loved music and he loved to play the harmonica. He used to sit me on his lap while he was playing the harmonica and patted his foot in rhythm with the music. I would clap my hands and hum to the melody, smiling with pride. He never had any training in playing the harmonica, but he could play Christian, country, jazz, and R&B music without missing a beat. I was really entertained when he tap danced across the living room floor. I remember Mama smiling when he tap danced over to her and kissed her on the cheek. She blushed, embarrassed I had seen them in passionate behavior.

I remember Daddy counting his coins on the coffee table to buy me a flute for my music class in school when I was in fifth grade. The frown on his face showed he didn't have enough money to purchase it.

"Don't you worry, he said. You're going to have your flute if I have to go without a meal."

The following weekend at the grocery store, I noticed that Daddy didn't buy the same items for his lunch. He purchased peanut butter and a box of saltine crackers instead of ham, bologna, bread, fruit, fig cookies, mayonnaise, and mustard. The following Monday through Friday for two weeks, he carried peanut butter crackers and a thermal bottle of water to work for lunch. I was so excited when I received my brand-new red and white flute, and I felt blessed to have a daddy that sacrificed his lunch for me to have it. It felt good to be like my music classmates and I made sure I received a "very good" on my report card in music. Daddy was proud that I had learned the flute and happy that I played the flute while he played the harmonica. We were a good musical team.

Daddy was very proud. He would always feed me before visiting his friends or family because he didn't want to give them the impression that I was hungry. Also, he wanted to make sure that if his friends or family insisted on me eating, I wouldn't eat too much. He was smart and he knew what he was doing. I couldn't eat anything because I was full from eating Mama's delicious food. One day we went to visit Daddy's sister, Aunt Katie, in Mebane, North Carolina. Mebane is located mostly in Alamance County, with a portion in Orange County. It was a nice getaway place at a short distance to go for fresh air, relaxation, trail walks, fishing, camping, and delicious home-cooked meals. I was always excited to go to Aunt Katie's warm and beautiful country home, partly because, in my opinion, she was the best cook in town. She always wore a beautiful homemade apron and a hairnet when she was cooking, washing dishes, or cleaning. She enjoyed cooking and feeding people, and she cared about the appearance of the meals she served. Her homemade meals and snacks were always colorful and neatly arranged on the table with cloth napkins, forks, spoons, knives, and beautiful glasses and a pitcher for beverages. Her table arrangements could have won first place if entered in a contest, or could have been on the cover of *Southern Living* magazine.

When we walked into her house one day, I smelled homemade butter cookies baking in the oven. The large cookies were shaped like stars, Christmas trees, angels, candy canes, and reindeers. She gave me a hug and guided me straight to the table to enjoy myself. She poured me a glass of milk and left the rest up to me. I didn't stop eating cookies until Daddy gently stepped on my foot after noticing I had eaten all the cookies on the platter but one. Filling me up with Mama's delicious food didn't work that day. Daddy didn't waste any time on the way home telling me how disappointed he was about my behavior.

"Lord have mercy, you should be ashamed of yourself."

"What did I do, Daddy?"

"You know what you did. You ate almost a dozen cookies. I can't believe it. We fed you a full course meal and candied yams for dessert to make sure you wouldn't be hungry. A lot of good that did. I've never been so embarrassed in my life. Don't be calling your mama or me when your stomach starts hurting."

"I'm sorry, Daddy, I couldn't help it."

"What do you mean you couldn't help it? Yes, you could help it. You weren't hungry. You were being greedy."

"Those butter cookies were so good, I couldn't stop eating them. I tried to stop, but it didn't work."

"Young lady, if you eat like that again at someone else's house, we won't take you with us to visit again. Do you understand what I just said?"

"Yes sir."

Mama smiled at me. "She will do better next time. She's not used to eating butter cookies."

In spite of his disappointment, I didn't regret eating the cookies. They were well worth the scolding I got from Daddy. Two hours after arriving home, I began having stomach pain and made several trips to the bathroom. After using the bathroom several times, my stomach pain subsided. I didn't call on Daddy and Mama, and I learned my lesson about overeating. Soon after we visited Aunt Katie's house, ingredients for butter cookies were added to the grocery list. I was excited when I smelled Mama's butter cookies baking in the oven. They were big, round cookies topped with different colors of homemade butter icing. Mama had created her own butter cookie recipe and they were absolutely delicious. Soon, I was making butter cookies like a professional. The next time Aunt Katie invited us over and had butter cookies as a snack, I only ate one cookie. Even today, butter cookies are my favorite dessert and I love the buttery smell throughout my house when they're baking.

9

Fried Fish and Buttermilk Biscuits

I hated going fishing with Daddy at Buds Island, North Carolina, but I enjoyed the long ride on his big truck viewing the beautiful trees and blooming bushes and flowers, learning the history of the area, and meeting prominent people that made a "positive difference" in the city. Before we left for our fishing trip, Mama cooked a hearty breakfast for us and had our food bags on the kitchen table ready for us to take on the trip. She also had two thick homemade cushions in a coarse sack to take with us. Mama made sure we had plenty of food to eat by packing peanut butter crackers, cheese straws, fried chicken biscuits, ham biscuits, apples, plums, and water. Her crackers, cheese straws, and biscuits were homemade, and the apples and plums were homegrown. Eating Mama's food was the best thing about the fishing trip.

Daddy wore bib overalls, a long-sleeved shirt, and a straw hat, and I wore a skirt, a long-sleeved blouse, and a big straw hat to protect me from the hot sun. I was never allowed to wear slacks or shorts, regardless of how hot or cold the weather was.

"Daddy, why do you sit here all day just to fish when you can go to the store and buy it in a few minutes?

"The fish in the grocery store can't touch the fresh fish I catch in the lakes. The grocery store fish are tiny, don't look right, and sure don't taste like the fish I catch. Besides, fishing relaxes me and feeds my family for at least several months. I feel good catching fish for your sweet mama, seeing her smile when I come home, and helping her clean and freeze the fish.

She loves fish and it's my gift to her. When I was a little boy I was taught to fish because fish was all the meat we had to eat. We had fish with grits for breakfast, fish biscuit and pinto beans for lunch, and fish and fried potatoes for dinner. I never got tired of fish."

"In the good book, in John 6:1–5, fish was the meat Jesus multiplied to feed people who were hungry. Jesus went to the other side of the Sea of Galilee. A lot of people followed him because they had seen him heal the sick and work miracles. When Jesus finally got up to the mountain, he sat down and watched the people gather around him. Jesus wanted to feed all the people. He asked Philip where were they going to buy bread for all the people to eat. Even though Jesus knew what he was going to do, he wanted to test Philip. Philip told Jesus that six months of money wouldn't buy enough food for the all the people to eat. One of the disciples, Andrew, said to Jesus, 'There is a boy here who has five loaves of bread and two fish.' I bet all those people said to themselves, How in the world are five loaves of bread and two fish going to feed all those people? Jesus took the loaves and fish, thanked the disciple, and fed over five thousand people until they were full. When the people saw the miracle Jesus had done, they told everyone that he was a prophet and that he was born into the world to help all the people. Jesus let them know he would give them what they needed if they trusted in him. You know, those people were happy. I bet you they were shouting and praising his name. Anything that Jesus does is good."

"Wow, Jesus can do everything!"

"He does everything that is good for us."

"He will feed us too."

"Yes, he will make sure we have what we need."

"We eat a lot of fish."

"Fish is good for your brain. Daddy told me that fish makes you smarter."

"Really?"

"It's true. I know he was right because look at how smart you are, Edna."

I chuckled and appreciated fishing for the first time. After sitting for hours, Daddy began catching medium-size fish. It was amazing to see how he had control of his fishing pole when pulling the fish out of the water.

"Look at all these fish I've caught. This is enough for a few dinners."

"It's a lot of fish to clean."

"Your mama and I can clean these fish in no time. We've been cleaning fish for a long time."

"I don't know how to clean fish."

"Do you want to learn how to clean them?"

"That's alright."

"I thought you would say that."

Daddy winked his eye at me and smiled. Daddy knew I had a problem with seeing him cut into the fish's bellies and removing all the entrails. It was disgusting to watch. Every time they cleaned fish, I almost vomited. After many unsuccessful attempts, they excused me from helping them clean fish.

"Daddy, are you ready to go home?"

"Do you mind if I catch one more fish before we leave?"

"No sir."

Fishing all day wasn't one of my favorite pastimes, but seeing Daddy happy made me happy. He got a thrill out of catching fish, no matter how small or big they were or how many he caught. It was something electric about the fish hitting the baited hook that excited Daddy. He would jump up and down like a little boy who just got his first pet. Fishing was the only time I saw Daddy with that much energy and enthusiasm. How could I say no to him? It was his fun time to escape to a peaceful and quiet place to relax his mind. Thank goodness the shade trees protected me from most of the sunlight and the cushion saved my bottom from getting sore.

Catching one more fish wasn't as simple as I thought it would be, as I realized when I saw Daddy struggling with the pole. The force from the shaking fishing pole almost pulled Daddy into the water. Daddy didn't let go of the pole, even though he slid a couple of times from the force of something wrestling with the pole. His determination was not going to let him give up.

"Daddy, don't pull it anymore! You going to get hurt!"

Daddy didn't respond or look back at me. He kept his eyes on the fishing rod and he kept his foot firmly on the ground. Suddenly, a powerful strength grew within Daddy and he swung the fishing rod out of the water with no problem. When I saw the huge fish on the hook flapping, I started running up the hill near the maple tree.

"Edna, where are you going?

"The fish is trying to get away. Come on Daddy, get away from it."

"Don't you worry, everything is going to be alright. Come back down that hill before you step on a snake. Your mama will have a fit if you get bitten by a snake."

Daddy knew what to say to make me come back down the hill. Snakes frightened me and I wasn't going to take the chance of being bitten. When I came back downhill, I noticed the huge fish had stopped flapping and was lying on the ground next to the water bucket that held the other fish. Daddy tried to put the fish into the bucket of water, but it wouldn't fit. Daddy poured all the ice from the cooler into the sack the cushions were in. He put the fish in the iced sack and carefully placed it in the back of the truck. Happiness came when Daddy packed up everything else and we headed back home.

"Lord have mercy, I'm glad this day is over."

"A rough day, huh?"

"It was okay until you caught that big fish. When I saw that big fish on your fishing pole, my heart started beating fast. Thank God the fish didn't pull you into the water."

"Yes, I thank God too. My fishing rod is stronger than I thought it would be. There isn't anything better than a good strong fishing rod.

"Why do you need a strong fishing rod?

A strong fishing rod is needed when catching fish because you never know what size or type of fish will bite the bait. If the rod isn't strong, a big fish could break it. This fish was really big. Even I was surprised when I saw it on my hook. It's the biggest fish I have ever caught!"

"It's a good thing you bought a good one."

"Uh huh."

"Mama is going to be surprised too."

"Yes, she will. We will get up early tomorrow morning and clean fish. Hopefully Willie will fry fish and bake bread for dinner tomorrow."

"We're just going to eat fish and bread?"

"We won't be able to eat anything else. You know how we love to eat fish. We don't stop eating until it's all gone."

I shook my head in agreement and we both started laughing simultaneously. Daddy was right. We never had one piece of fish or one biscuit left after a meal. Mama's fried fish was the best I had ever eaten and there was no one I knew that could make biscuits better than Mama.

On the way home, I fell asleep in the middle of Daddy's conversation about a lake in Wilmington, North Carolina, where he could catch more fish to freeze. Trying to keep my eyes open didn't work because I was extremely tired just from watching Daddy catch fish and from sitting out in the sun. The aroma of cinnamon and hot chocolate woke me up the next morning. I realized Daddy hadn't woken me up when we'd arrived home the night before. He had carried me into the house and put me in my bed with all my clothes on except for my shoes.

Before taking my bath, I entered the kitchen, where I found Daddy and Mama eating cinnamon bread and drinking hot chocolate. She had a plate set for me. When I came to the table and sat down, she cut me a slice of cinnamon bread and poured me a cup of hot chocolate.

"Did you rest well last night?"

"Yes ma'am."

"Good. Herbert said you were tired."

I yawned.

"Daddy caught a big fish yesterday."

"Yes, he did. And he caught a lot of medium-size fish too. We have a lot of fish to eat for a while."

"It's a lot of fish to clean."

Herbert and I cleaned the fish this morning. The fish is in the freezer, except for the big fish. We're having the big fish for dinner today."

"Did y'all clean all the fish?"

"All of it," said Daddy. "Willie don't play when it comes to cleaning fish. It was hard for me to keep up with her."

"Herbert did just fine. He scaled all the fish, helped me clean the fish, and cleaned up afterward."

Mama looked for opportunities to praise Daddy and never said anything negative about him. She always talked about his wonderful qualities and his commitment and loyalty to her. She never complained about things Daddy couldn't afford to give her but was thankful for what he was able to provide for his family.

"Thank you, Willie. I'm going to fry the fish for dinner. All you have to do is make the bread."

"Thank you, Herbert."

It was obvious that when Mama praised Daddy it built him up and strengthened his commitment.

At noon, Mama was making biscuits while Daddy was outside making preparations to fry fish. He lit the fire and heated the cooking oil half an hour before he tested it. He sat a big cast-iron pot on a metal rack he had placed on the open fire. While the cooking oil was heating, he took the fish out of the water and patted it dry on both sides with a towel. He sprinkled a little bit of salt on both sides of the fish and battered them with self-rising flour.

"Daddy, why isn't the pot full of hot oil? It's half full."

"Because when you add the fish to the cooking oil, the cooking oil will rise and spill out of the pot into the fire."

"Wow."

"Guess what happens next?"

"What?"

"The pot catches on fire and we get burned."

"And the burn will hurt us?"

"It will burn your skin off."

"Oh my goodness! I'm glad you didn't fill it up."

"You don't have to worry the least little bit. I know what to do to keep an outside fire from spreading. One way is to not cook outside if you don't know what you're doing. And you can't be scared of the fire. It make sense to fry fish for a long time before frying fish in an outside fire. Next time, I will show you how to fry fish in a frying pan on the kitchen stove."

"After I fry fish in a pan for many years, I will be ready to fry fish in a pot."

"Yes, you will be ready then."

Daddy sprinkled a little bit of flour in the cooking oil to test for frying. The oil passed the test when it started sizzling. Daddy carefully dropped one fish at a time into the hot cooking oil and used a long-handled metal strainer to remove the fish. The fish was golden brown on both sides and the crispiness was just right. We had a wonderful time laughing and talking at our private family fish fry. The fish didn't just look good, it was seasoned perfectly and it was delicious with Mama's golden-brown buttermilk biscuits. There were so many pieces of fresh fried fish that came from the big fish. It was amazing how much food we had to eat. Daddy asked me to say the prayer.

"God is great, God is good, and God, thank you for our food. Amen."

Eating fish and biscuits at the dinner table reminded me of the story Daddy had told me about Jesus multiplying two fish and five loaves of bread. Daddy didn't have the magic to multiply bread and fish, but he sure could fry some good-tasting fish. There were no leftovers. We ate all the fish and biscuits. Mama's homemade lemonade was the icing on the cake.

Fishing became an adventure to me and a beautiful memory I will never forget. Every time we went fishing, I thought about how Jesus fed five thousand people with just two fish and five loaves of bread. Nothing we face on earth is too big for God. The next summer, I went fishing with enthusiasm, even though it took me all day to catch one fish. Daddy helped me hold on to the fishing rod. It was a big fish! It was almost as big as the fish Daddy caught the previous year. Daddy also taught me how to fry fish in a frying pan on the woodstove. Soon after I got the hang of frying fish, he taught me how to make chopped barbecue and homemade slaw. On every fourth of July, we enjoyed a meal of fried fish, chopped barbecue, home-made slaw, and buttermilk biscuits. Today, I have no desire to fish, but fried fish is still one of my favorite foods. Because eating healthy is important, I only eat fried fish once in a while. If I want fresh fish, I purchase it in the seafood section at Harris Teeter. Unfortunately, I'm too scared to fry fish in a pot on an open fire, and I very seldom fry fish in a frying pan at home. Burlington is blessed with several restaurants specializing in seafoods, and their fried fish are always golden brown. My favorite restaurant is Hursey's Bar-B-Q. As far back as I can remember, Hursey's Bar-B-Q, a family-owned restaurant, has offered delicious seafood platters on their menu, including fried fish and chopped barbecue. It's my favorite restaurant because their fried fish and barbecue taste just like Daddy's and Mama's. Harbor Inn Sea-food and Mayflower are my next-favorite seafood restaurants to eat out. There is never one piece of fish or one hush puppy left on my plate from any of these three restaurants. Daddy was smarter than a lot of people gave him credit for. Studies have proven that fish is good for the brain, and eating it regularly reduces the risk of Alzheimer's disease.

10

He'll Be Home Soon

My life was turned upside down when I overheard Mama and Daddy talking about him going to work in another state. I couldn't tell my parents I heard them talking because I would get in trouble for listening to grown-up conversations. I had sleepless nights wondering when Daddy was going to talk to me. My headaches didn't make the situation any better, nor did having the feeling of anxiety and fear of getting picked on. My small classmates of single parents were bullied more often than my classmates with both parents. The bullies were known for name-calling, pushing, and threatening by yelling, "What you gonna do? You don't have no daddy!" The thought of them knowing Daddy wouldn't be home made me sick to my stomach. Without a doubt, I knew I would be a target for bullying because I was skinny and shy. Wishing and hoping Daddy was bluffing didn't last very long. Finally, after waiting a few weeks, Daddy had a family discussion before moving to Norwalk, Connecticut for almost a year to earn enough money to provide for his family.

"Daddy, why do you have to go?"

"I'm not making enough money to pay the bills, and the money I have in the bank is almost gone. I can't have your mama working. Her job is to take care of you and the house."

"I can get a job to help."

"That's mighty sweet of you, Edna, but you have to go to school and help your mama around the house. I won't be gone long."

"There must be something you can do to pay the bills. Mama's brothers will help."

"I don't want anyone taking care of my family and I don't want anyone in my business. I'm the man of this family and it's my responsibility to take care of y'all. A man is supposed to work and not beg. It's in the Bible about a man working for his wife and children. If I don't work for my family, I have disobeyed Jesus and I'm just as bad as a person that doesn't believe in him. So if people want to talk about me because I'm trying to find a better way to take care of my family, let them talk. I'd rather they talk about me for trying than talk about me because they had to pay my bills."

Early the next morning, Mama and I helped Daddy pack his clothing, food, and water. He kissed us goodbye and drove out of the driveway into the main road with his head out the window, waving. I didn't understand why Daddy had to move to another state to pay the bills and take care of us. Later, in my older years, I realized it was hard for African Americans to find good-paying jobs in the South. I cried all night for Daddy and wondered if I would ever see him again. Mama assured me that Daddy would never let anyone or anything stop him from coming back home.

"Your daddy has to do what he has to do. He's tired of worrying about how he is going to take care of us. Don't you worry. Everything is going to be alright. Your daddy will be back home soon whether he makes money or not. He can't stay away from us for long."

After Daddy left, Mama wasn't the same. She didn't have her happy, confident smile and she didn't have the energy she once had. She would go to bed early and sleep late into the morning. She didn't talk as much and many times I saw her wipe tears from her eyes when I walked into her room to see if she was alright.

"Mama, are you crying?"

"No, darling, I'm not crying."

"Don't worry, Mama. Daddy will be home soon."

"I'm not worried at all about your daddy coming home. Your daddy misses us as much as we miss him. He couldn't stay away from us if he tried. We're a family and God will keep us together forever."

Mama wrapped her arms around me and kissed me on the cheek. She quickly got off the subject so I wouldn't ask any more questions. When I became a wife, I understood what Mama was going through without Daddy. She missed Daddy holding her at night and whispering sweet words in her ears. She missed having him to talk to and she missed his selfless leadership.

Mama never stopped reading her Bible and she never stopped praying. Every night she would pray and thank God and his son Jesus Christ for loving us, for letting us wake up each morning, for food to nourish our bodies, for a roof over our heads, for health and strength, and for keeping Daddy safe.

The bullies got a big surprise when they started bullying me. My courage had built up and I was ready for them. Little did they know I had practiced throwing rocks to hit my target, speaking up for myself without cursing, exercising to tighten my arm muscles, and making strong, tight fists. There was one girl who loved bullying my friends because she enjoyed seeing them cry or run because they were afraid of her. The day I saw her push one of my close friends to the ground, I was determined I was going to give her a taste of her own medicine. The opportunity came one day while walking home from school with my classmates. It seemed like she came out of nowhere, huffing and puffing in my face. My friends stepped back, trembling from fright. With her hands on her hips, she gave me a mean look directly in my eyesight. She immediately started calling me names, and she kept moving closer to me until her chest was touching my chest. She pushed me, but I didn't fall because I used my strength to stand firmly on the ground. Before I knew it, I had shoved her to the ground and enjoyed every minute of it. I warned her that if she or her bullying friends bothered me or my friends again, she wouldn't be able to get up or walk again. My friends circled around her with their hands on their hips. They gave her an angry stare. She got up from the ground and ran off, not looking back. We hugged and made a promise to each other that we wouldn't take any more bullying. Daddy once said that some things are better left unsaid, and that's exactly what I did. I never told my parents what happened that day because they wouldn't have approved of my actions. My courageous friends and I became like the three musketeers: "One for all, all for one." We were loyal to each other, especially in times of trouble, but we never had another problem with the school bullies.

Daddy communicated with us on a regular basis. I remember Mama running to answer the telephone to talk to him, almost knocking over her treasured, antique Sheraton Cherry and Bird's-Eye side table. She was so happy after she talked to him and she had the biggest and brightest smile I had seen on her face in several days. A burst of energy came out of nowhere and she wanted to clean everything in the house. Mama would go into another room to read his letters, and she never missed telling me that Daddy said he loved me and would be home soon. The day he came home was one of the best things that had ever happened to me. I fell several times running to the end of the long gravel road to meet him. He picked me up and swung me around. Best excitement ever! I hugged him tightly and didn't want to let go. He kissed me on the cheek almost a hundred times. It was the first time I saw him kiss Mama on her lips and the first time I saw him hold Mama in his arms publicly. At that moment they didn't care who saw them and they didn't care if no one approved of their behavior. They were truly in love with each other.

We were so excited when Daddy told us we were moving to the city to another house. He wanted us to be closer to our doctors, hospitals, grocery stores, retail stores, gas stations, and city parks for family activities.

"We're going to move to a smaller house for right now, and later we will move to a bigger house as soon as I have enough money saved for a down payment."

I didn't care where we moved to as long as we were with Daddy. I knew he would take care of us and I was excited I could walk downtown to different stores.

We moved into a small, white wooden house surrounded with caring, giving, and loving neighbors. Every one of them had outstanding cooking skills and I wasn't shy eating whatever they offered me to eat and drink. I always ate at my neighbors' houses because if I took the meal home, Daddy would be angry. He maintained his pride and dignity. The attic in our small white house was my favorite getaway when I wanted to play with my baby dolls, read, or dress up in Mama's dress and her high heels. I had two red-oak desk chairs and a table to do my homework without interruptions. During my studying time, Daddy would come up to the attic to make sure I wasn't playing. The attic had become disorganized and in disarray because I didn't have anything to put my belongings into.

"This room is a mess."

"I know, Daddy. I don't know what to do with my stuff. I don't want to throw anything away."

Daddy was so sweet to purchase a used trunk for the attic to store my dolls, toys, tea sets, kaleidoscopes, paper dolls, games, and small stuffed animals. I knew Daddy would take care of the problem, as he always did.

At an early age, Daddy talked to me about my future and boys.

"I want you to go to college to be a nurse, he advised. I don't want you having problems paying your bills and depending on someone else to take care of you."

"Your education is important and it is something nobody can take from you."

"Stay away from those sweet-talking boys and keep your britches up and your dress down."

He was serious about his conversations with me and never talked to me in a harsh tone. He always ended our conversation with positive comments.

"You're so smart and you can do anything. I'm proud of you and I know your mama is proud of you too. Who knows, you may be the president of the United States one day."

Daddy cared about our health and believed in doctors. I remember that when I was a child he explained to me why it was important for me to go to a doctor. I didn't want to go because I was afraid of getting a sting from a shot or having a stranger examine me.

"You're going to love Dr. Scott. He is nice to everyone, including 'colored people.' All he cares about is taking care of his patients."

Daddy drove us to Scott Clinic in his shining Ford car and I had to sit still to keep from wrinkling my clothing. He wanted his car and his family looking good because he wanted to be respected. I had to stay outside and play without getting dirty until the nurse called for me to come inside to be seen by Dr. Scott. The nurse took me to the examination room while Daddy and Mama waited patiently. Every time Dr. Scott came into the examination room, he would pick me up and sit me on the examination table. Boy was he strong! His caring smile validated what Daddy had said about him. I felt safe in his presence and it was evident that the color of my skin wasn't an issue with him. Every clinic visit, Mama gave Dr. Scott eggs, bread, or vegetables to show our appreciation for him caring for us. After I finished my clinic visit, Dr. Scott's nurse gave me vanilla ice cream. I wanted to go to see Dr. Scott every day just to get ice cream. He was always very detailed when explaining the medication he had prescribed, and he loved us as his own.

"Make sure you take your medicine. I want to keep you here for a long time."

Dr. Scott did home visits and he checked in on Mama on an ongoing basis when she was sick to make sure she was okay. He shook Daddy's hand every time he came to our home, and he talked to Daddy alone after each visit. Daddy thought the world of Dr. Scott because he respected him as the head of his household, and he valued Daddy's input in his family care. Daddy didn't trust any other doctors and he would call Dr. Scott when he had questions about his family's condition or the medication we were taking. Dr. Scott never ignored Daddy and always answered his questions. Dr. Scott gave Daddy credit at the clinic because he didn't want money to stop us from coming to our regular appointments. Dr. Scott set up monthly payments for Daddy and his monthly payments were whatever Daddy wanted to pay. Daddy never missed a payment.

"Your word is your bond."

Daddy chose the best doctor in town. Dr. Scott was just like a family member and he always talked to me after seeing Daddy or Mama. At the end of his conversation he would say,

"Now, I want you to do good."

"Yes sir."

I felt beautiful and special. He was like an uncle to me and a brother to Daddy. Daddy and Mama bragged about Dr. Scott after each visit, and it was obvious they were pleased with him because he had our best interest at heart. One of the reasons I wanted to be a nurse was because of the experience I had at Dr. Scott's clinic. It was an environment where everyone cared for each other and they treated everyone the same. They worked as a team with their remarkable abilities to heal people from all walks of life. I respect doctors, health-care providers, and nurses to the upmost. They have a big job! As I grew older, I realized I was too compassionate to be a nurse, but I knew without a doubt I wanted to work in a health-care environment. I was employed in the health-care system for forty-two years in administration. I enjoyed taking care of patients indirectly and staff directly. I know Daddy and Mama would be proud of the love and service I have given to humanity.

11

Forgiving Miss Clara

Something strange happened to Mama one day on a summer evening while we were shelling peas. Mama stopped talking in the middle of a sentence and fell sideways in her brown armchair with her head slumped. Daddy called out her name several times, but she didn't respond. He quickly picked her up and rushed out the front door, heading toward his car. I started screaming "Mama" in hopes she would answer me. I ran out the front door behind Daddy with the intention of going with him, but he wouldn't let me ride with him.

"I'm taking your mama to the hospital. You can't go. Go back in the house and stay there until we come back home. Don't forget to lock the door when you close it."

I could tell by Daddy's facial expression and the tone of his voice that he was worried about her diagnosis and if she would recover from it. Frightened, I stood at the door and watched Daddy drive down the road at high speed without stopping at stop signs or lights. He was going so fast that I could barely see his car because of the dust from the dirt road. I closed the door, locked it, and took refuge in my bedroom to escape from the situation. Getting under the bedcover and falling asleep was my escape from dealing with Mama's sudden illness. After I woke up from sleeping a couple of hours, I ran to each room in the house, determined to find Mama. She wasn't home. Leaning against the living-room wall, my frustrated emotions slowly surfaced again.

"Mama isn't home because she's at the hospital."

There was nothing I could do to change the situation. My denial was replaced with realization. I began having negative feelings about the outcome of Mama's illness and what was going to happen to me. I sat on a brown floor pillow by the front door and waited impatiently. For some unexplained reason, I became emotionally attached to the pillow because Mama had made it for me and I felt connected to her. Soon, I fell asleep in a fetus position. After hours of sleep, I was awakened by the squeaky noise of the front door closing. Every light was on in the house when Daddy came home late that night. Mama wasn't with him. Daddy went to every room of the house except the living room and bathroom and turned the lights off. He came back into the living room, sat down on the sofa, and looked at me. I sat up but didn't move from the floor pillow. My stomach cramped and my heart began racing. My legs were so weak that if had I tried to get up, they probably wouldn't have been able to support me. I was thinking the worst, but when I saw the sparkle in Daddy's eyes and his caring smile, it was obvious that Mama was alright. That day was the first time I had seen him tear up in spite of him trying to hide it.

"Dr. Chandler operated on your mama and she made it through her operation. Thank God! They did a good job and she is resting now. She will be home in a few days and we have to make sure she takes her medicines every day. I called Dr. Scott after the operation and he came to see your mama. He looked at her chart and talked with Dr. Chandler about the operation. He said no one could have done a better job than Dr. Chandler, and he said I got her to the hospital in time. Hallelujah! After she leaves the hospital, he will be coming to the house to check on her. For a while, she won't be able to do any housework or cook, and she will need plenty of rest. She doesn't need to worry about nothing. Edna, she will need all of our help."

"Yes sir."

"When she comes home, you will see a bandage in the middle of her head when you comb her hair, but no one else will be able to see it because her thick, long hair will cover it up. Dr. Chandler had to shave a small spot of hair off her head to take care of the problem, but they promised me she will heal soon. While she's in the hospital, Miss Clara will be staying in the house with us to do the cleaning, laundry, ironing, cooking, freezing, and canning to help us out. Willie can rest better knowing everything is taken care of. Miss Clara will be here tomorrow morning before I leave for work. I won't get back until late because I will be with Willie until she goes to sleep. Be good to her and do what she tells you to do."

"Yes sir."

Mama had bushels of peas that needed shelling and freezing, and she had a few jellies, jams, pickles, and vegetables she hadn't finished canning for the winter. Frankly, I wasn't too happy about having Miss Clara stay with us while Mama was in the hospital, but we needed help. Miss Clara was in her early sixties, was known throughout the neighborhood as a caregiver to anyone that needed her, and was active in our church and in fundraising for community needs. She was very short, obese, unattractive, and grumpy. Her Machiavellian behavior at fundraising events and church functions kept me at a far distance from her. She lied on people just to get her way and she didn't care whose toes she stepped on to get ahead. She had helped out in many homes when someone was sick and she had the reputation of doing a very good job. Most of the adults loved and believed in her, but their children disliked and were afraid of her. The next morning when I woke up, Daddy had left for work and Miss Clara was in the kitchen cooking breakfast.

"Good morning, Edna. Did you rest well last night?"

"Yes ma'am."

"Good! I won't have to hear any excuses about being tired or not feeling like doing anything today. Right?"

I didn't understand why she was talking to me that way when I hadn't complained about my chores. I answered the question with no animosity.

"Yes ma'am."

"We have a lot to do today before Herbert gets home tonight. After you eat, I want you to finish shelling the peas for freezing."

I frowned.

"Do you know how to freeze peas?"

"No ma'am."

"You will know today because I'm going to show you."

"Okay."

After eating breakfast, I washed dishes and swept the kitchen floor while she watched me. She pointed her index finger toward the floor near the stove.

"Sweep over there again! You didn't sweep the crumbs off the floor! I don't know how you missed it."

"Yes ma'am."

I swept the area over again and hurried to the living room to finish shelling the peas, hoping she would come and help me. Instead, she stayed in the kitchen and began canning the cucumber pickles. From the living room, I could hear jars popping, cabinet doors slamming, pots hitting the floor, and her huffing and puffing.

"Lord have mercy, please help me."

I was suffering and in need of Mama's sweet personality, love, and hugs. I missed her so much and I wanted her home as soon as possible. My fingers ached from many hours of shelling peas and my stomach was growling because I hadn't eaten since breakfast. It was three o'clock and I had to go to the bathroom.

"Where are you going?"

"To the bathroom."

As I walked to the bathroom, I noticed an empty, used plate and glass on the kitchen table. A chicken leg, fried fatback, a biscuit, and a half ear of corn were on a serving dish on the table. I couldn't believe Miss Clara had eaten and hadn't offer me anything. After using the bathroom, I confronted her.

"I'm hungry. Can I have a piece of chicken and a biscuit?"

"When you finish shelling the peas, you can eat."

Miss Clara had overstepped her boundaries. She wasn't going to keep me from eating food Daddy had purchased. Determination kicked in, and I headed toward the table.

"You better learn to do what I tell you to do! You're going to have to listen to me, young lady, whether you like it or not. Your mammy ain't coming back home."

"Yes, she is too! You don't know what you're talking about!"

"Don't you holler at me, young lady. You had better start getting use to me because your mammy is going to die. Now, get back in the living room and finish shelling those peas, hardhead."

Before I knew it, I had snatched the serving dish off the table, stepped on Miss Clara's foot as hard as I could, and run out the kitchen door toward the wooded area in the back of the house. She was screaming and crying. She gave up trying to stop me. She couldn't catch up with me because she was overweight and out of breath.

"Oh my God! My foot is broken! I'm calling your daddy! You're gonna get a whooping. You just wait and see. I'll show you who's the boss. Stay gone! I'm not staying another day at this house with you. You're nothing but the devil!"

The wooded area was my comfort zone when I wanted to be alone. It was my place of peace, meditation, prayer, and uninterrupted silence to sift through my thoughts or stressful situations. When I reached my favorite resting spot by the huge maple tree, I sat down on the ground and ate my meal. The fresh air and beautiful trees relaxed me and I was going to stay put until Daddy came home.

"Daddy will find me. I'm not going back in the house with Miss Clara until Daddy comes home."

After sitting in the woods for what seemed like an hour, I became fully aware of my bad behavior.

"What have I done?"

Daddy and Mama had taught me to respect the elderly and to listen to them because they were wiser. Even though Miss Clara wasn't nice or wise, I was feeling guilty for stepping on her foot.

"Why did Mama have to get sick? This wouldn't have happened if Mama was home. Now, I'm in trouble because of Miss Clara. She is going to tell Daddy a lie on me. Daddy might not believe me when I tell him what happened. Oh God, please don't let her foot be broken. Oh my goodness, she's probably crying because her foot is hurting. I want to go and help her, but I'm scared of her. She hates children. What am I going to do, God? Maybe I need to run away. No, I can't run away. They will miss me. Mama, please don't die. Miss Clara said you're going to die. God, please let Mama get better so she can come home."

Exhausted from crying, I had drifted off to sleep when I heard Daddy calling my name.

"Edna! Edna! Where are you?"

"I'm over here, Daddy."

When I saw him coming toward me, I began crying hysterically. The look on his face showed anger and I knew a scolding was going to come, or a spanking. There was no way out of what I had done to Miss Clara and there was no way I was going to stay in the same house with her. The moment had come for me to tell my side of the story and I wasn't going to sugarcoat it. Daddy was going to know exactly how I felt about Miss Clara before we left the woods. If he made me stay with her, I had no choice but to run away.

"What in the world is going on? Miss Clara said you wouldn't listen to her and you stepped on her toe."

With a raised voice, I began telling my side of the story.

"She didn't tell you what she did with her lazy self. She sat around the house and didn't do nothing. All she did was eat and tell me what to do. She wouldn't give me anything to eat and she said Mama was going to die! I hate her and I'm not going back in the house with that mean old woman again. I will stay out here until Mama comes home."

"Calm down. You don't have to worry, she will not be coming back. Let's go back to the house and I will tell her we don't need her anymore. You need to apologize for stepping on her toe because you were wrong. Two wrongs don't make a right."

"Yes sir. You're not going to spank me?"

"No, but if you do it again I will."

"I will never do it again!"

"Good."

"Is Mama coming back home?"

"She will be home in a few days. Don't pay any attention to what Miss Clara says. She doesn't know what she's talking about. Miss Clara is a decent and hardworking person but her words don't come out right when she gets angry. She's had a rough life and she makes everyone pay for it. She's a little rough around the edges."

"What does 'rough around the edges' mean?"

"She's not polished and she needs some work done on herself to help her get along with people. She probably needs to go to finishing school."

"What is finishing school?"

"It's a school that teaches people how to talk to each other and how to be a lady or gentleman."

"Yes, she needs to go to finishing school and stay there!"

Daddy chuckled.

"Well, she won't be coming back to the house anymore. She messed up this time with her choice of words. Since we won't have Miss Clara helping out, we're going to have to work extra hard to take care of things while your mama is in the hospital."

"Okay. I will work real hard."

Daddy took my hand and guided me through the woods and back to the house. He had held my hand many times, but my hand had never felt as good as it felt that day. The way he held my hand reassured me that he hadn't changed his love for me and I was still his little girl. No longer did I feel stressed or afraid of Miss Clara because I knew Daddy wouldn't let anyone harm me. When we arrived at the house, Daddy looked at me. His look told me what I needed to do.

"I'm sorry, Miss Clara, for stepping on your foot."

"It's okay, Edna. I know you miss your mama."

I couldn't believe she acted so innocent in front of Daddy. She didn't care about Mama or anyone else but herself. Other than wanting to punch her, I wanted to tell her to stop faking, but I knew Daddy would make me apologize again. It was a revelation of what my friends had experienced with her, but Daddy was different than most parents. He couldn't be persuaded by anyone, no matter who they were.

"Edna, go to your room. I have to talk to Miss Clara."

Slowly, I walked to my bedroom looking at Miss Clara. When I passed her standing by the window, I rolled my eyes at her and quickly closed the door.

"Ain't no telling what they're talking about," I thought.

I tried to listen to their conversation by leaning my head against my bedroom door, but all I heard was mumbling. When Daddy called me out of my bedroom, Miss Clara was leaving out the door with her pocketbook.

"Thank God she's gone."

Daddy never said another word about Miss Clara or my behavior. Oh, how amazing Daddy was with conflict and how blessed I was to have a father that had my best interest at heart. No one could measure up to Daddy—I wouldn't have traded him for all the money in the world. He believed in me and acted in a humble manner without hurting Miss Clara's feelings. What an awesome daddy! As days passed by before Mama came home, Daddy, family members, and friends completed the canning and freezing of the food left. Close family members helped me keep the house clean and Daddy made sure our stomachs were full with cold-cut sandwiches and farm milk. It was a hallelujah day when Mama came home and a day for prayer and thanksgiving. With emotion, Daddy took us to God in prayer.

"Dear God, thank you for healing Willie and bringing her home to us. You know how much she means to us and I don't know what we would do without her. She's a good wife and mother. She has faith and trust in you. She loves everybody and there isn't anything she wouldn't do to help someone. Thank you so much for loving us. We love you too and we trust you with all our hearts. There is nothing greater or stronger than your love, and we're nothing without you. Amen."

Soon, Mama was up and walking again with her usual activities, house responsibilities, and prayer meetings. Daddy was back at work, and I was doing my best to make sure Mama didn't go back into the hospital by doing extra chores and helping her cook. She was amazed at my eagerness and determination to make sure our house was clean and comfortable. Months after the incident, I changed my feelings and attitude toward Miss Clara. Thanks to God, I forgave her for her actions. One year later, I went with Daddy to visit her at her home. He said I needed to go with him to see her. She was critically ill. When we arrived, she was lying in bed with family around her. Her eyes lit up when she saw me and she reached her hand out to me. She smiled weakly at me when I held her hand and kissed her on the cheek. She and I didn't let go of each other's hands until it was time for me to leave.

"Goodbye, Miss Clara. I love you."

Did I love her, or did I say it to make her feel better? It was a combination of both, plus compassion and empathy for a person that was well loved by the community in spite of her flaws. Daddy was wise and a peacemaker. He knew exactly what he wanted to accomplish when he asked me to come with him. He knew she was critically ill and he wanted to achieve a positive closure between Miss Clara and me before she died. It was obvious we had forgiven each other. She died peacefully a month later. Miss Clara's purpose in my life was to teach me forgiveness. Throughout my life I have been lied on, cheated, talked about, and mistreated, but I have forgiven all the people who have done these things. I pray that if I have mistreated anyone, I will be forgiven too. Unwillingness to forgive hinders prayers: "And when you stand praying, forgive if ye have ought against any; that your Father also which is in heaven may forgive you your trespasses" (Mark 11:25). Forgiveness sets you free and gives you peace of mind.

12

Centraneta

A little four-legged bundle of joy weakly wandered into the backyard of our house when I was hanging clothes on the line. She looked malnourished, and her dirty white hair was sticking to her body from the past few days of rain. She brought warmth and comfort to my heart when she leaned against my leg. We had never had animals in our house before and my parents had never given an opinion on having pets. Several of Daddy's friends took their dogs with them hunting, but none of them owned a kitten, including my friends. The kitten's eyes looked sad, watery, and weak. When I reached down to pick her up, she came to me with no hesitation. She was skeletal, her vertebrae and shoulder blades were visible, and her bones were protruding. Her skin was red, scaly, and dry, and she was scratching herself to relieve the itching.

"Poor little kitty cat. Don't you worry. We have food in the house and water to drink. Let's go into your new home. You don't have to worry about being hungry again."

Love came instantly—a biological connection I had never experienced before with an animal. She was the missing link in my life that gave me tenderness, nurturing, and sensitivity to the needs of others. Also, having her gave me a feeling that went beyond any selfishness or self-interest. My desire was to have a positive effect on her well-being. She was alone and needed someone to love and protect her. When she looked directly into my eyes, she became my baby and I became her mother. Immediately I hurried into the screened-in porch, grabbed the dented dishpan out of the trash can, and rushed into the kitchen to bathe my kitten. She was so soft and cuddly. After washing the kitten and wrapping her in a towel, I fed her milk and Mama's homemade beef and gravy. She almost choked from eating and drinking too fast.

"Don't eat too fast, kitty. Nobody is going to take your food from you. You're my only baby and you don't have to worry about a thing. I'm not going to let anyone hurt you."

After laying the kitten down on a pillow, I heard Daddy and Mama coming in the front door. They had been outside on the front porch painting the front-porch chairs.

"Oh my goodness, what am I going to do?"

Mama came out on the porch first, and Daddy followed behind her. Daddy and Mama looked down at the kitten and then at me. Daddy made a facial expression indicating he wasn't pleased, and Mama didn't make any expression at all. They were both silent for about fifteen seconds before they began asking questions and voicing their concerns. Mama asked the first question and voiced her concerns.

"Where did you get this kitten?"

"She came in the yard to me all by herself."

"Do you think you can take care of her? It's not an easy job."

"Yes ma'am, I can do it."

Mama gave a sigh.

"There are a lot of responsibilities for taking care of a kitten. You have to feed her, clean up behind her, give her a bath, and walk her. You can't walk off and leave the responsibility on someone else."

Mama looked at Daddy for him to join in on the conversation. Daddy walked over to the kitten and stared at her for a few seconds. He scratched his head and turned toward me. Tears flowed down my face.

"She was hungry and I didn't want her to die! Please don't make me give her away! She needs me!"

Mama and I watched Daddy walk back and forth on the porch several times before stopping. He walked over to the kitten and picked her up. Daddy never showed compassion for any animals and had a strong belief that animals should be kept outside. When he picked up my kitten, I held my breath, praying for the worse not to happen.

"Oh God, please don't let Daddy throw my kitten outside in the yard. Please don't let him make my kitten leave."

Daddy gently rubbed the kitten's back just like a mother would rub her newborn baby. He looked at her in the eyes and rested her head on his shoulder. He continued rubbing her back until she fell asleep. Daddy's gentleness and sensitivity toward my kitten surprised me in a good way. Daddy actions revealed his love and compassion for animals too.

"Did you feed the kitten?"

"Yes sir."

"She looks like she hadn't eaten a good meal in a long time. She doesn't have to worry about food now. You're going to make sure she eats good every day, right?"

I smiled at Daddy. "Yes sir."

"Did you give your kitten a name?"

"No sir."

"Well, it's time for you to name her. You can't own a kitten without a name."

"Oh my goodness! I can keep her?"

Daddy looked at Mama with a smile, and then he looked back at the kitten lying patiently in his arms. Mama came over to Daddy and looked at the kitten, softly rubbing her head. They both said yes simultaneously, but Daddy added a condition to the agreement.

"If someone claims her, you will have to give her back to the owner."

"Yes sir."

Daddy put the kitten back on her pillow and gave me a serious look.

"It's time to give the kitten a name. Don't give her a name you can't spell."

Before I knew it, a name came out of nowhere. It was a name I had never heard before and didn't exist until I made it up for my sweet kitten. In my opinion, she would be the only kitten in the world with a name that represented strength and beauty.

"Her name is Centraneta. It is spelled C-e-n-t-r-a-n-e-t-a. The e's and the a's are both short vowels."

Daddy knew I had made up the name and spelling, but he couldn't say anything because I had used the short vowel sound and pronounced Centraneta correctly. Daddy and Mama praised me with pride.

"There's nothing wrong with dreaming up a name for your animal. Wow! You did great with the spelling, vowels, and how you said 'Centraneta.' It proves you can do anything if you want to."

Mama smiled at Daddy and chimed in on the conversation.

"What a sweet and precious name for your kitten. Centraneta has a caring and loving person to take care of her. She's blessed to have you."

"Thank you, Mama and Daddy. I love her."

Daddy and Mama went back into the house to give me privacy with Centraneta.

Weeks went by and Centraneta adapted to her new surroundings. She adored me. She was the prettiest and whitest butterball kitten I had ever seen. Her weak walk had changed to a strut. After each bath, I would spray Mama's honeysuckle cologne on her neck and stomach to make sure she didn't have an animal odor. While I was enjoying Centraneta, Daddy was looking for her owner.

"Gosh, Daddy! Why do you have to keep asking people if Centraneta is their kitten? If they cared about her, they would come looking for her."

"It's the right thing to do. Wouldn't you want your kitten returned to you if she ran away?"

"My kitten wouldn't run away."

"Why not?"

"Because I would feed her. Animals don't run away from home if you feed them. She ran away because nobody fed her. She had lost a lot of weight. She probably would have died if she hadn't found us. Please don't send her back."

"You love her, don't you?"

"Yes, I do, and she loves me. If you send her away, she will come back to me. She knows she's safe with me."

"She is that indeed. Don't worry. Everything should be alright."

Weeks and several months passed, and Centraneta was still with me. Daddy and Mama gave me permission to move her from the screened-in porch to my bedroom because the weather was too cold for her to stay outside. She had become part of our family, and I made sure she had everything she needed. I did extra chores and sold soda bottles at the local mom-and-pop store to earn extra money to buy her cat food and milk. Soon she enjoyed taking baths and loved playing in her bath water. When she was outdoors, she wouldn't walk in the mud, but enjoyed walking in the rain on the grass. My friends enjoyed playing ball with her. She loved small, bright, colored balls. We would take turns throwing the ball across the floor for her to run after. The laundry-basket game was her favorite game and my favorite because it gave me freedom to do other things while she played. It kept her occupied and in the same location for a long time, which gave me time to entertain my friends. I would turn the laundry basket upside down with a ball underneath. She spent several hours sticking her paws through the holes in the basket to get the ball. She was so cute when she became frustrated after being unsuccessful. She looked up at me for help, and I didn't hesitate to get the ball for her. She also loved chasing my metal train across the floor. She was faster than the train, and she stopped it every time I rewound it. The train game only lasted for a few minutes because I was tired of rewinding it. She encouraged me to engage in more active play with her throughout the week. She kept me busy nonstop, so I was exercising without realizing it. I would race her up and down the hallway and pretend to look for her when she hid under the bed. She made me laugh more than I had ever laughed before. She was smart and very observant. She also had a tender and soft side. She loved to be cuddled, and I loved cuddling her. Cuddling Centraneta took my mind off things that had bothered me in the past, which was therapeutic and much needed. When I held her next to my chest, her purring sound made me relax and fall asleep sometimes during the day. No matter what I had going on, I took full responsibility in caring for her. Before leaving for school, I set bowls of water, milk, and cat food in her room. Mama was home during the day and enjoyed kitten-sitting while I was at school, but I felt it was necessary to make sure everything was in place for Centraneta while I was away. I wanted Mama to enjoy Centraneta without stress. Mama was always singing or humming gospel music to Centraneta when I came home from school. Having Centraneta as her companion during the day made her happier and more relaxed. When Daddy came home from work, he always asked Mama how her day was with Centraneta. He wanted to make sure Centraneta wasn't a burden to Mama. Afraid Mama might give a negative answer, my stomach cramped each time he asked.

"How was your day with Centraneta?"

"It was good. She's a good kitten. She doesn't bother me a bit. She is so quiet, I had almost forgotten she was in the house. She scratches the door when she has to poop and pee, and she goes back to Edna's room when she's finished. She loves music. Her eyes light up when I sing or when she hears music on the radio. When I turn the radio off, she stares at it and then at me, waiting for me to turn it back on. Ha, ha, ha, ha, ha. She's something."

"She's going to be the only Christian kitten in town."

Mama rolled her eyes at Daddy and began shaking her head.

"I can't believe you said that."

Daddy chuckled and went to my room to check on Centraneta.

Mama always had many sweet stories to tell about her day with Centraneta, and she told them with enthusiasm. It was a blessing how Centraneta changed our household in a good way. Soon I stopped worrying about what Mama's answer would be to Daddy. She loved Centraneta.

One late evening when I was reading a children's story, Daddy came into my bedroom and sat in the chair next to my bed. Centraneta was on the floor in her homemade bed next to me, eating cat food and sipping water.

"Edna, Centraneta is yours to keep."

"Really?"

"Yes."

I jumped out of my bed and started jumping up and down on the floor. There were no words to describe how happy I was when no one claimed her. She was mine to keep forever! In a comfortable position, Centraneta tucked all four of her feet under her body and curled her tail around. She looked up at me and purred. She must have known she had a home forever that was full of love and compassion. My wish had come true!

Centraneta wasn't allowed to ride in the car when we visited relatives or when we went on a joy ride just to get out of the house. Whenever I was wearing a coat or sweater, I would hide her and take her with me. I was the last one to get in the car and the first to get out of the car to keep from exposing her. She didn't move, nor did she meow, purr, chirrup, growl, chatter, or hiss. She acted like she knew we would be in trouble if Daddy and Mama found out she was in the car. During the ride, I would periodically unbutton my sweater or unzip my coat to give her light and to make sure she wasn't suffocating. She would look up at me and lay her head back on my chest with contentment and trust. I could tell she knew she was in good hands by her body movements and caring eyes. I spent many joy rides with my parents praying she didn't poop or urinate in my lap. Hiding the smell or trying to explain the wet car seat to them would have been hopeless and a prayer wouldn't have saved me from being disciplined. In spite of all the dilemmas, I couldn't leave Centraneta at home alone. The secret rides we had together are memories I will cherish forever and never forget.

Summer arrived and Centraneta had become more independent and secure in our home. Because of her gentle ways and learning through trial and error, my responsibilities for her had become easier. I learned how to work smarter, not harder. Juggling household chores, studying, taking care of Centraneta, and earning money had become manageable. Because of the warm temperature, she was moved back out onto the screened-in porch to her designated area with no hesitation. She was a good kitten no matter the circumstance. She accepted change better than I did. She was comfortable and territorial with her food, water station, and litter box. She no longer felt vulnerable while eating, drinking, or eliminating. She wasn't fearful anymore if she heard a car coming in the driveway or if a visitor went onto the porch conversing with Daddy or Mama. She kept eating and drinking without jumping or moving from fright. Without me, she would run around loose outside and climb up and down the same tree. She loved hiding from me behind the huge magnolia bush near our house and she enjoyed chasing butterflies throughout the yard. After she finished her activities, she would come back onto the porch to her resting location, tired out. She always took a quick nap after her outdoor activeness. Before praying one night, I had several questions for Daddy.

"Daddy, did God create animals too?"

"God created everything."

"Is there anything in the Bible about animals?"

"Of course there is."

"Can you read it to me?"

Daddy picked up the Bible, thumbed through some pages, and began reading: "'Then God said, "Let the earth bring forth the living creature according to its kind: cattle and creeping thing and beast of the earth, each according to its kind; and it was so,"' Genesis 1:24. 'For every beast of the forest is Mine, And the cattle on a thousand hills. I know all the birds of the mountains, And the wild beasts of the field are mine,' Psalm 50:10–11. God created everything that moves, including Centraneta. You might think you own Centraneta, but she is not actually your kitten. She belongs to God, but he picked you to give her the love and care she needs. He knew you would do a great job and you have done just what God expected of you. I know God is pleased. You have made your mama and me proud. Keep up the good work."

"Thank you, Daddy. I feel better now."

"Were you worried?"

"Not really. I just wanted to make sure God loved Centraneta too."

"I'm glad you feel better."

After my conversation with Daddy, my burdens were lifted. Centraneta and I resumed our new daily activities with more energy than before.

Centraneta learned to ride peacefully in my red wagon as I explored and hunted in the woods for treasures. She enjoyed the snacks in the wagon and loved hanging her head off the side of the wagon, looking down at the insects on the ground in wonderment. Other than already having won Mama's heart, she won Daddy's heart too. When he arrived home from work every day, she would run up to him and sit on his shoe. She wouldn't leave until he talked to her and rubbed her back. In spite of how tired he was when he arrived home, he gave her attention for a few minutes. I was surprised at how Daddy baby-talked to Centraneta and Centraneta made funny sounds back at Daddy. Mama's consistent love, gentleness, and caring soul was one of the major reasons I could give Centraneta the life she deserved. Centraneta had it made. She was spoiled by all of us. She gradually matured physically and behaviorally, but her dependence on me never changed. I wouldn't have had it any other way. Taking care of her, protecting her, and giving her unconditional love was amazingly rewarding. It was a miraculous feeling that was indescribable.

Two more years of joyous moments playing and taking care of Centranetta came to a halt when I noticed something different about her. Her weight loss, cloudy, filmy eyes, and extreme weakness in her hind legs were the first signs of her illness. Gradually, her interest in eating decreased and she didn't interact with me as usual. Her stools were diarrhea and she began eliminating outside of her litter box all over the floor. When I threw her favorite ball to her, she wouldn't run after it. She slept more than usual and behaved as if she were in pain. I knew she was critically ill when I held her and she didn't snuggle up to me. She cried and tried to bite me and was no longer excited when she saw me. She wanted to be alone. I cried so many nights because she was sick and I couldn't do anything to save her. She was my baby and it was my responsibility to make her feel better. I felt I had failed her. Daddy and Mama checked her breathing on an ongoing basis and made sure she was comfortable. I laid on the porch next to her each night before going to bed. She didn't move, but she didn't take her sad eyes off of me. She was helpless and afraid. I didn't ask Daddy and Mama any questions about her illness because I knew what their answers would be. I could feel in my heart what was happening to my sweet Centraneta. She was dying, and I didn't want to accept it. My sweet baby was going to leave me unless God intervened. I said the same prayer every night.

"Dear God, please don't let Centraneta die. She doesn't want to leave me. Please make her better."

Mama woke me up one warm Saturday morning by kissing me on the cheek. Daddy was standing behind her with his head in a downward position. I quickly sat up in my bed, raising my eyebrows. Mama sat down on the bed close to me and gave me a warm hug.

"Edna, Centraneta has gone to heaven."

I jumped up from my bed and ran to the porch where I had left her the night before. There she was—alone and still, wrapped up in her blanket with her eyes shut. When I touched her, she was cold and stiff.

"Centraneta! Centraneta! Centraneta! You have to wake up. You can't leave me. No! No! No! Please! Please! Please! I need you!"

Mama pulled me away from Centraneta and Daddy picked Centraneta up from the floor and headed down the back-porch steps.

"Where are you taking Centraneta? Leave her here! She is going to wake up. Please don't take her away."

"Edna, your daddy is going to have to bury Centraneta."

"Nooooo!!! She is going to wake up. Please believe me."

Daddy stopped on the last step, walked back onto the porch, and laid Centraneta down.

"Edna, there isn't anything we can do to save her. She was sick and tired, and she was ready to go home. You were good to her and you made her very happy. She was the luckiest cat in the world. You were a wonderful little mother to her and I know she appreciated all your kind deeds to her. She loved you and she wouldn't want you to get sick. You have got to calm yourself down. You have so many good memories of Centraneta. Now your mother and I are going back into the house for a few minutes to leave you alone with Centraneta. After you finish talking to her, we're going to give her a proper burial."

I made sure Daddy and Mama were nowhere in sight when I began talking to Centranetta, weeping and wailing.

"Centranetta, I wish I could've saved you. I tried so hard. I hope you're not mad at me. You're the only cat I will ever love and I promise I won't get another cat. You don't have to worry about another kitten or cat taking your place. If a kitten or cat comes into my yard, I'm not going to take care of it. I'm going to tell Daddy to take it to someone else's house."

Since I refused to stay at home, Daddy allowed me to pull Centraneta in my wagon to the wooded area where she was going to be buried. I squatted down to the wagon to cover her face with a piece of pink and white fabric Mama had given me. I didn't take my eyes off of her while Daddy was digging a small grave.

"Edna, do you want me to put her in the grave or do you want to do it?"

Hesitantly, I took her out of the wagon, almost tripping over a rock nearby. My eyes were full of tears, but I was determined I was going to be strong and do it myself.

"I'm going to put Centraneta in the grave. She's my responsibility."

Daddy stepped back from the grave without saying another word. Mama walked over to a patch of flowers nearby. Slowly I walked to the grave and put her into it gently, crying hysterically. Daddy picked me up and held me tight, still not saying a word. I cried until I couldn't cry anymore. Daddy put me back down at the grave site. I took a few deep breaths to make sure I was calm enough to do one more thing for Centraneta. I reached into my pocket and pulled out her favorite ball and laid it in the grave beside her.

"I love you, Centraneta. You're with God now. He loves you too."

I straightened out her blanket and the cloth on her face. I looked up at Daddy and stepped back from the grave for Daddy to shovel the dirt into it. After Daddy had shoveled all the dirt into Centraneta's grave, Mama gave me a handful of flowers she had picked to plant on Centraneta's grave.

"Edna, do you want me to help you?"

"Yes ma'am."

There was no way I was going to say no to Mama. She loved Centraneta too and she did a good job taking care of her while I was in school. Mama helped me plant the colorful flowers all over Centraneta's grave beautifully. She didn't stop picking flowers until she had covered the entire grave. There was something extra special that day walking back home in the middle of my parents. Daddy was holding my left hand and Mama was holding my right hand. Even though that day was the worse day of my life as a child, I was no longer afraid because of my caring and loving parents.

That night I interrupted Daddy's reading with a question.

"Daddy, why did Centraneta have to die?"

"Remember when I told you that Centraneta belonged to God?"

"Yes sir."

"Centraneta had served God's purpose on earth and God brought her back home."

"What was her purpose on earth?"

"Well, one of her purposes was to come into your life to teach you a different type of love. You worked hard to make sure she had what she needed. You became a better and more responsible person after Centraneta came into your life."

Trying to hold back my tears was difficult. All I could think about was Centraneta and how much I missed her.

"Edna, Centraneta will always be in your heart. God teaches us many things in ways that no one can explain, but everything God does is good. God does everything in his own time to prepare us to live in heaven forever. The good book says, 'To everything there is a season, and a time to every purpose under the heaven: A time to be born, and a time to die; a time to plant, and a time to pluck up that which is planted; a time to kill, and a time to heal; a time to break down, and a time to build up; a time to weep, and a time to laugh; a time to mourn, and a time to dance; a time to cast away stones, and a time to gather stones together, a time to embrace, and a time to reframe from embracing,' Ecclesiastes 3:2. The Bible also says, 'And God shall wipe away all tears from their eyes; and there shall be no more death, neither sorrow, nor crying, neither shall there be any more pain: for the former things are passed away,' Revelation 21:4.

"Nobody is going to die one day?"

"That's right. When we go to heaven we will live forever."

"What do I have to do to get to heaven?"

"You know the answer to that question. You were taught in Sunday school how to go to heaven."

"Believe Jesus died for our sins."

"Right."

"Ask for forgiveness."

"Right."

"And don't sin anymore."

"Right. The Bible will teach you to do what's right."

I was excited that I was going to see Centraneta again in heaven. I knew she was going to be in heaven because she had done everything right. In spite of my sorrow over the loss of Centraneta, I slept peacefully.

"Good night, Centraneta. I know you're watching over me."

I kept my promise to my sweet Centraneta. I have owned many pets in my life, but I have never owned another kitten or cat. There is no kitten or cat that could ever replace Centraneta, no matter how trained, cuddly, loving, or beautiful they are. I can never get Centraneta out of my mind.

She has a special place in my heart forever, and my love for her will never change. When I look back at my life with Centraneta, I have so much to be thankful for that I had somehow overlooked. It's unfortunate that for years I forgot the way my wise parents stepped back to let me grow independently, experience life challenges, and be there for me during the hardest time of my young life. Daddy stepped out of his comfort zone and gave me permission to take care of a malnourished, homeless kitten in need of some loving care. He gave me sole responsibility. He was always against animals living in people's homes and wouldn't eat at anyone's house that had an animal living there. Not only did Centraneta live in our house during the winter, Daddy helped feed her when she was a kitten while he was eating dinner. Compassion replaced his stern personality. He broke every rule he'd had in the past regarding animals, and he made new rules to ensure that Centraneta's health and welfare was intact. He never said he loved Centraneta, but his smiles and playfulness with her revealed his true feelings. He checked her food supplies on a weekly basis and he reminded me to purchase more when her supply was low. He was pleased when she gained weight and he would tell her how healthy she looked when he thought no one was listening. Mama had no problem saying she loved Centraneta, and her actions spoke louder than her words. She treated Centraneta like her child and did extra special things for her "sweet baby." Mama enjoyed sewing Centraneta a variety of beautiful, colorful pillows to sleep on and matching blankets to cover her up. Mama was so gentle and patient with Centraneta. Daddy and Mama praised me when I did a great job of taking care of her, and they encouraged me not to give up when I thought I was failing. Their support during the illness, death, and burial of Centraneta was healing and therapeutic. They had taken me out of depression in a consoling way. Daddy didn't throw Centraneta off some dirt road like she was nothing; he gave her a respectful, grave-site burial. He carefully dug her grave without me asking, and he let me lay her to rest. He had my best interest at heart. In my eyes, he was the greatest man on earth. Oh, how I wish I could tell him how amazing he was. Mama's thoughtfulness to pick white lilies for Centraneta's grave gave me understanding of and feeling for others, and respect for all burial sites. Mama knew I was heartbroken, and she knew exactly what to do to ease my pain. The flowers were a symbol of my personal memories of Centraneta and of my hope that she rest peacefully. Through prayer and my wonderful parents giving me extra love during my mourning process, I was able to heal mentally and move forward without the impact of childhood trauma. The cause of Centraneta's death was never known. Years later, I understood why Daddy didn't want me to own an animal. It wasn't because he was cold-hearted; it was because his budget wouldn't allow him to take a pet to the veterinarian when it was ill. He must have decided it was better for me to try to take care of Centraneta than to send her away and let her die. Centraneta was more than a cat to me—she was a godsend and a gentle living force that loved me unconditionally. Daddy was right, as usual. Centraneta came into my life to make me a better person. Because of her, I learned to give, appreciate life, take care of others, sacrifice, forgive, understand, see the beauty in others, and love deeply as if there's no tomorrow. God is amazing! He taught me about life through loving experiences with Centraneta. She definitely served her purpose.

13

Thanksgiving Guest

"Is it not to deal thy bread to the hungry, and that thou bring the poor that are cast out to thy house? When thou seest the naked, that thou cover him; and that thou hide not thyself from thine own flesh?" (Isa 58:7). This is what Daddy practiced and taught me when he felt like it was needed. In our home each year, Thanksgiving was a time to give thanks to God and celebrate our appreciation with food, songs, discussions at the dinner table, and "praising his glorious name." Daddy and Mama sometimes included a few unfamiliar faces to eat Thanksgiving dinner with us if they had nowhere to go. The church members planned months in advance before Thanksgiving by raising money from selling fish and chicken plates and collections from community donations to make sure the less fortunate had food to eat on Thanksgiving Day. The hospitality women church members would do the grocery shopping and use the church kitchen to cook for the families. Each household would receive a fresh-baked turkey, candied yams, potato salad, green beans, stuffing, giblet gravy, cranberry sauce, homemade biscuits, corn bread, and sweet tea. Every Wednesday morning before Thanksgiving, I went with Daddy and Mama to church to help box up meals for the families. The church was very organized by arranging all the food that went into the box in a row. Each item was carefully wrapped in aluminum foil, and boxes were checked twice to make sure nothing was missing. To make our jobs accessible and quick, the boxes were placed in front of the Thanksgiving meals to keep us from walking back and forth for boxes. After the meals were boxed, the men took the boxes outside and loaded them onto the back of their trucks. A list of the families and their addresses were given to the driver so he could take the food to their homes. After we had cleaned the kitchen and packed up our utensils, pots, and pans, we went home to start our Thanksgiving dinner. Daddy participated in the preparation of Thanksgiving dinner by keeping the fires burning in the fireplace and the woodstove, squeezing the lemons for lemonade, placing the heavy, dressed turkey in the oven and taking it out when it was done, bringing canned vegetables down from the attic, and driving to the store to get items we were out of. Family members peeled potatoes and apples, oiled the baking pans if needed, put all the cooking ingredients from Mama's list on the table to make it easier for her, transferred the dirty dishes and utensils from the table to the sink to be washed, and cleaned the house. My job was to help family members clean up the house, wash dishes, and set the table on the day of Thanksgiving. Mama did all the baking and cooking. She gave us the joy of tasting the cake batter, and she made an extra layer of chocolate cake for us to eat the day before Thanksgiving. It was so good with a glass of cold milk. Holidays were the times we had an abundance of food to eat and I ate everything in sight. Mama always had Thanksgiving dinner ready a day in advance, and on Thanksgiving Day she added her final touches to bring the holiday in. She decorated the kitchen with her homemade Thanksgiving kitchen curtains, towels, tablecloth, table mats, and napkins. The beautiful eighteenth-century tableware consisted of dinner plates, saucers, bowls, and glasses. The white porcelain Thanksgiving dinner plates, saucers, and bowls were bordered with a harvest of oak leaves and acorns in autumn colors. In the center of each table mat was a turkey artfully embroidered in seasonal colors. Although much smaller, the same design was on the right side of each clear drinking glass, giving the table an elegant appearance. Using our own imaginations, we decorated the front porch with a wagon wheel flourishing with dried vines and flowers attached to it, and an old, unfinished wooden wagon filled with autumn leaves and small pumpkins. The pumpkins were never used for Thanksgiving dinner. We hated pumpkin pies. Mama made sweet potatoe pies instead, and after Thanksgiving, the pumpkins were given to our church to make pumpkin butter. There is one particular Thanksgiving that is unforgettable because of the magnitude of Daddy's love, kindness, and giving heart to everyone, even in the worst situation. On that Thanksgiving morning, Daddy read these verses from the Bible:

But this I say, He which soweth sparingly shall reap also sparingly; and he which soweth bountifully shall reap also bountifully. Every man according as he purposeth in his heart, so let him give; not grudgingly, or of necessity: for God loveth a cheerful giver. And God is able to make all grace abound toward you; that ye, always having all sufficiency in all things, may abound to every good work: (As it is written, He hath dispersed abroad; he hath given to the poor: his righteousness remaineth for ever. Now he that ministereth seed to the sower both minister bread for your food, and multiply your seed sown, and increase the fruits of your righteousness;) Being enriched in every thing to all bountifulness, which causeth through us thanksgiving to God. (2 Cor 9:6–11)

While Daddy was reading, I was trying to figure out what was going on in his mind. To get a point across, Daddy always found a verse in the Bible to validate his message. He was smart enough to know that no one would disagree with him if his words came from the Bible. After reading the Bible verses, Daddy began a serious conversation with us.

"Today for Thanksgiving, we are going to have a person eating with us who is homeless. His name is Milton. I knew he had been living on the street because I saw him walking on the side of the road with a bag on his back stuffed with clothes. Sometimes when I passed him, he was sitting on the side of the road eating from a can. Something was bothering me about this man so I stopped on the side of the road and talked to him. It took him a while to open up to me, but he finally did. He has no family, doesn't make enough money to rent a place to live in, doesn't go to church, lives in the woods during the summer and abandoned buildings in the winter, and you will know as soon as he walks in the house that he hasn't taken a bath in a long time. Your mama said it was alright for me to ask him to come to dinner. Nobody should be alone at Thanksgiving. We're supposed to give, no matter how little we have. It's pitiful and a shame when people don't help each other out. He said when he asked for help people wouldn't help or give him work to do, but they talked about him. Because of how people treated him, he doesn't want to go to church. Thank God, that problem has been taken care of. I'm going to pick him up in a few minutes. He trusts me and I want to make sure he is treated like family. When he comes here for dinner, don't be staring at him but be nice. We're going to talk like we used to, and we're not going to skip over him when we go around the table to tell what we're thankful for. Understand?"

"Yes sir."

"I'm proud of you for understanding. I'm going to get him now. He's got some cleaning up to do before dinner, and he needs someone to talk to. I enjoy talking to him. It took him a while to talk to me, but now he talks to me about everything. If you listen to him, you can tell he is a good and smart man. He thinks about things that make sense. Things that a lot of people don't think about. He's been through a hard time. He just didn't know which way to turn to get himself back on the right road again. Because he has been alone and doesn't have family or friends he doesn't feel comfortable talking to strangers. Edna, please don't ask him questions."

"I won't, Daddy."

"The reason I'm bringing him here to eat dinner with us is he needs to know somebody cares about him. Being around caring people is good for his soul. It's a shame he was going to sit in the woods on Thanksgiving Day. Lord have mercy." From the look on Daddy's and Mama's faces, it was obvious they were happy about Milton coming to eat with us. It was the Christian thing for them to do, and they always enjoyed blessing people no matter who they were or what their situation was."

When Milton entered the living room, it was obvious he didn't have anyone. My first observation of him wasn't good because of the hair on his face and the clothing he was wearing. His clothing was badly soiled and torn, the soles on his shoes were coming off, and the long hair on his head and face hadn't been washed or brushed. His hands and nails were dirty, and the plaque buildup had almost destroyed his teeth. The awful body and mouth odor he brought into the house was almost intolerable, but his soft, intelligent voice and his demeanor gave evidence of a kind and gentle man. These were my thoughts in so many words:

Maybe he was struggling because of personal issues or situations from the past that had never been resolved.

Maybe he didn't have positive people in his life and he didn't feel comfortable asking for help.

Whatever the reason, he was down on his luck and he needed someone like Daddy in his life. Daddy needed people like Milton in his life because he was the happiest when he could ease the suffering of others. He always helped others privately, and he wasn't pleased when he heard people bragging or talking about someone they had given to. His actions reflected the Bible: "Therefore when thou doest thine alms, do not sound a trumpet before thee, as the hypocrites do in the synagogues and in the streets, that they may have glory of men. Verily I say unto you, They have their reward.

But when thou doest alms, let not thy left hand know what thy right hand doeth: That thine alms may be in secret: and thy Father which seeth in secret himself shall reward thee openly" (Matt 6:2–4).

Milton's personality was pleasing, but his attire and body odor made me feel uncomfortable around him. His shyness, looking away from us, one-word answers, crossing his arms, flinching, and scratching his nose was evidence that he wasn't comfortable with himself. After introducing Milton to us, Daddy and Milton left the living room, with Mama behind them. When Daddy and Mama left the room together, something was going to happen, good or bad. Since Milton was with them, I knew it was going to be good. When they were gone from my sight, I cracked open the windows in the living room and the kitchen. Even though it was chilly outside, fresh air was needed in the house to get rid of the odor as much as possible. All I could think about at that moment was the mouthwatering smells of delicious food, and I couldn't let the bad odor of Melton's body and mouth ruin our holiday dinner.

"Lord have mercy, we can't hurt his feelings. Daddy will be angry. What do I do? That smell has to go."

My prayer was answered about an hour later when Mama returned to the kitchen.

"Mama, where are Daddy and Mr. Milton?"

"Your daddy was cutting Milton's hair. We should be ready to eat shortly. Milton's taking a bath now."

"Were you helping Daddy?"

"I was ironing some of your daddy's clothes for him to wear."

"Is Daddy still with Mr. Milton?"

"Yes, he is. Milton doesn't feel comfortable unless he is close to Herbert. He asked Herbert to stand by the bathroom door while he's taking a bath. Bless his heart."

"Can he wear Daddy's clothes?"

"They may be a little big on him, but they'll do."

"Did you find him some shoes?"

"No, I didn't. Do you know why?"

"Why?"

"Your daddy is good for stretching a penny. Last week Pic 'n Pay had a sale on shoes. If you buy one pair of shoes, you get another pair for a penny. He bought himself a pair of work shoes and Milton a pair for a penny."

"Daddy is good to everybody."

"Yes, he is. It doesn't matter how much or little we have, he is going to share it if someone needs it."

"Mama, you're just like Daddy. You share everything too."

"You don't miss nothing, do you?"

"Nope. I sure don't."

"Our friends and family share with us too. That's what God wants us to do."

Mama kissed me on the cheek and headed to the kitchen with me right behind her.

"Don't tell nobody. You know Herbert doesn't like people knowing his business."

"Don't you worry. I won't say a word."

Family members gradually came to the dinner table, chatting about favorite foods, Thanksgiving decor, favorite songs, fashions, hairstyles, and how things were going at school. The chatting stopped when Milton entered the kitchen. My eyes popped open because of his new, odorless, clean look. He was smiling, and he wasn't hanging his head down. Daddy introduced him to everyone, and everyone gave him a warm greeting.

Whew! I'm so thankful he took a bath and cleaned up.

I quietly closed all the windows and returned back to the kitchen where the family was gathered. Milton sat down at the dinner table next to me and looked over at Daddy. With his head up, he closed his eyes and placed his palms together. Daddy began praying.

"Dear God, thank you for waking us up this morning. Thank you for loving us even when we don't do what we should. Thank you for this meal we're about to receive in your name's sake to nourish our body. Thank you for blessing us with food to eat and being able to share with others. Thank you for blessing us with Milton to eat Thanksgiving dinner and to glorify your name with us. Bless Willie for preparing the food for us and the hands that helped her. Amen."

Mama had all the food beautifully arranged on the table, with gospel music playing on the radio on a table in the corner of the room. The food dishes were passed around one by one, and it was a delight to make a choice to spoon out a serving or reject it and pass it on to the next individual. No one was pressured to eat all of the dishes and no one was denied what they wanted to eat. There were four baskets of yeast rolls placed in the middle of the table for easy reach, and four pitchers of lemonade. Milton got a serving of everything that went around the table, but he had good table manners. He did everything I was taught to do when eating. He didn't eat anything with his hands, he didn't open his mouth until he had chewed and swallowed his food, and he didn't eat quickly. He complimented Mama with gratitude.

"Oh my God, Mrs. Brown, you can cook! I haven't tasted anything this good since I was a little boy. My mama used to cook just like this. This turkey, dressing, and gravy can win a cooking contest."

"Thank you, Milton. What a kind thing to say."

"I'm telling the truth. Lord have mercy, these rolls melt in your mouth."

Daddy started laughing and chimed into the conversation.

"You're right, Milton, my wife can cook. She can take a sack of flour, a bag of potatoes, and different spices and make one of the best meals you ever tasted. When she gets through spicing those potatoes in different ways, you got yourself something. She doesn't just make biscuits with the flour. She makes desserts, gravy, dumplings, cheese crackers, and pecan flapjacks. She didn't just cook the food on the table. She made the tablecloth, table mats, napkins, and the pillows in these dinner chairs. She can sew anything. She's not just a 'putty' face."

Daddy tickled me every time he said "putty" instead of pretty, and he made me proud when he bragged about Mama.

Mama blushed and shook her head. "Herbert, Milton has heard enough about me. Let's talk about something else at the table."

Daddy had to get a few more words in before stopping. "I'm telling nothing but the truth."

Milton nodded his head up and down, agreeing with Daddy. "And the truth will set you free," he said.

Milton was relaxed and felt free to voice his opinions. It was amazing how he joined in on the family conversations, laughed with us, told stories without being asked about his childhood life, and how much he looked up to Daddy. He agreed with everything Daddy said, and he praised the kind acts Daddy did for him and other residents in the area. It was gratifying to hear stories about services Daddy did for others without charging anyone a penny. In the middle of the meal, we carried out the tradition of giving thanks individually. That Thanksgiving was different, more heartwarming than the previous ones because Milton participated without hesitation, voicing a tearful speech that warmed my heart. I had great sensitivity to his problems, pain, and suffering, and his need for a family to love.

"I'm thankful for my life because there was a time I didn't want to live. So many things happened to me when I hadn't done anything to deserve it. My friends and family turned their heads the other way when I needed them the most. When I asked for bread and water, they gave nothing. I'm thankful I still love them. I was hungry, living on the streets, eating from trash cans, and sleeping in run-down houses that no one was living in during the winter to stay warm. Death was the only way out. I'm thankful for my mama and daddy for teaching me when I was a young boy that if I killed myself, I might go to hell. They told me to pray and God would give me all I need. After talking myself out of killing myself, I started praying. I didn't miss a day praying. God came to me one cold night with his arms open. I'm thankful I have God, and I will never let him go. He loves me and he takes care of me. Because of him, I have all I need to get by. He gave me Herbert, and I'm so thankful for him. He has done so much for me. He never looks down on me, and he treats me like a good brother. On his way to work, he stops on the side of the road every morning just to feed me. I'm so thankful for the cans of vienna sausage, potted meat, crackers, apples, and water he brought me. He wanted nothing in return. He never gave up on me. Herbert, you're a good soul. I'm thankful you gave me a good word to find a job. Because of you, I have a job cutting timber and helping out at Rocky Lake Farm, and I will get to live in the farmhouse and get paid for working. I won't have to sleep on the ground or in the cold anymore. I'm thankful for Herbert's family, who have treated me better than anyone except for Mama and Daddy. You let me come in your home, and I feel welcomed. I'm thankful for the delicious food and being able to eat Thanksgiving dinner on a table and in a warm house with a good family. It means so much to me. Thank you so much. So much good has happened to me and I owe it all to God."

My mind flashed back to verses Daddy had read to me from the Bible: "Heaviness in the heart of man maketh it stoop: but a good word maketh it glad" (Prov 12:25); "Pleasant words are as an honeycomb, sweet to the soul, and health to the bones" (Prov 16:24). Milton was living proof of how encouragement gives spiritual strength and courage to strive for the highest goals. Holding back the tears from coming down my face was difficult for me to do. I wiped my eyes with my hands, holding my head down so no one would see my face. At that moment, love and compassion for humanity developed. Sobbing, I got up from my chair and went over to Milton's chair and gave him a hug. He embraced me and kissed me on the top of my head.

"Mr. Milton, I'm so sorry people didn't help you and made you sad. Don't cry. Please don't cry. Daddy's going to make sure you're alright. You don't have to worry about nothing."

"You're a sweet little girl. Thank you."

Suddenly, I realized I had broken a household rule. I had hugged a stranger.

"Oh my God, I'm in trouble."

Much to my surprise, Daddy and Mama were smiling at me. It was obvious they were proud of me by the look in their eyes. When Mama gave me a caring wink, I was relieved.

"Thank God."

After a few seconds of quiet, Daddy spoke up.

"Milton, you're a good man and I'm happy I met you. I have learned so much from you. You have taught me a lot about life and people. You're our family and you're welcome here anytime."

"Thank you. I really enjoyed all of y'all and the food was the best I have ever tasted in a long time. I have to say this again. You're a good cook, Mrs. Brown."

"Thank you, Milton. I'm glad you enjoyed it. You're going to take some food home with you. I'm going to box up some turkey, dressing, candied yams, turnip greens, yeast rolls, and a jug of lemonade for you to take with you. You don't have to worry about what you're going to eat with. I'm going to put in your food box plenty of paper plates, napkins, cups, plastic knives, spoons, and forks. I'm so happy you have a place to stay and a job. God is good."

"Yes, he is."

Daddy and Milton spent the rest of the evening discussing different topics. Daddy played his harmonica and Milton clapped his hands and tapped his feet to the music. They shared stories and talked about God's grace, their future goals, and upcoming community activities that Milton would enjoy. The family members and I helped Mama clean up the kitchen, and we all were happy to box up a meal for Milton. We put enough food and utensils in the big cardboard box to last a week. Thanksgiving was more meaningful that year than any other because we had a special guest that needed more than a Thanksgiving dinner. He needed a few good friends, love, respect, acceptance, understanding, purpose, and a mentor. Seeing Milton smile when Mama gave him the big box of food to take home made me feel even more appreciative of my parents than ever. They gave unselfishly and with love. Daddy inviting Milton to the house taught me a valuable lesson about my image when dealing with people. Through Milton I learned that the clothes I wear and the way I groom myself makes a huge difference in what people think about me. It determines whether people trust, distrust, ignore, or listen to me. Because of Milton, I became adamant about speaking up when I disapproved of the way a person was treated. There was no way I could be selfish enough to put my own need to be comfortable above the needs of others. It didn't matter if I was at home, at church, at work, shopping, or at an outing, I would speak for righteousness, regardless of the consequences. If I didn't stand up for what was right, I would be just as guilty. Also, I'm proud of who I am because God wonderfully created me. I never let anything get me down for a long time. If rocks are thrown at me, I'll catch them and make succulent planters and sell them. If someone speaks badly about me, I get on my knees and pray for the backbiter because they make mistakes just like I do. Luke 6:42 says, "Either how canst thou say to thy brother, Brother, let me pull out the mote that is in thine eye, when thou thyself beholdest not the beam that is in thine own eye? Thou hypocrite, cast out first the beam out of thine own eye, and then shalt thou see clearly to pull out the mote that is in thy brother's eye." It is wonderful how the Bible tells us God's plan of salvation and what God requires of us. God is awesome! In my eyes, Daddy and Mama were angels taking care of people and helping those who were in crisis. Their ministering spirits never asked for anything for themselves. They worked together without disagreements, and their loyalty toward each other was surreal. They listened carefully and were attentive to each other, and they always spoke highly of each other. I heard Daddy telling Milton he needed a good woman like Mama. He talked about how sweet Mama was, her delicious foods, and how she took care of him and the household. Mama talked the same way about Daddy to her church members, family, and friends. Their effectiveness as a team was something hard to find, and they respected each other in a gentle and loving manner. Their union as husband and wife was cohesive.

> Wives, submit yourselves unto your own husbands, as unto the Lord. For the husband is the head of the wife, even as Christ is the head of the church: and he is the saviour of the body. Therefore as the church is subject unto Christ, so let the wives be to their own husbands in every thing. Husbands, love your wives, even as Christ also loved the church, and gave himself for it; that he might sanctify and cleanse it with the washing of water by the word, that

he might present it to himself a glorious church, not having spot, or wrinkle, or any such thing; but that it should be holy and without blemish. So ought men to love their wives as their own bodies. He that loveth his wife loveth himself. For no man ever yet hated his own flesh; but nourisheth and cherisheth it, even as the Lord the church: For we are members of his body, of his flesh, and of his bones.

For this cause shall a man leave his father and mother, and shall be joined unto his wife, and they two shall be one flesh.

This is a great mystery: but I speak concerning Christ and the church. Nevertheless let every one of you in particular so love his wife even as himself; and the wife see that she reverence her husband. (Eph 5:22–33)

It's a mystery how I had forgotten how my parents had touched Milton and so many other lives, including mine, in a positive manner. Their love for each other was true, and it stood the test of time. Their strong bond was the happiness of having found affection toward each other. Because God was in their marriage, no one and nothing could separate them. It was definitely a beautiful union God had joined together: "What therefore God hath joined together, let not man put asunder" (Mark 10:9).

Milton quickly became supervisor over several employees of Rocky Lake Farm. Daddy was never jealous of Milton's achievements because he was satisfied with what God had given him. He was proud of Milton, and he wanted the best for him. He bragged about Milton to us all the time.

"I knew he had it in him. He's a smart man. Milton can do anything if he puts his mind to it. He just needed a chance to prove himself. I'm so thankful Milton didn't lose his faith in God. He joined the church and he's singing in the choir. I didn't know he could sing that well. Boy, he surprised me. I tell you, God is good."

Mama chimed into the conversation. "Yes, God is good all the time."

In one year, Milton built his own home on two acres of given land, and he married Hilda, a Sunday school teacher and upholsterer. Hilda was pleasant to everyone she met. She was strong, emotionally stable, mature, and selfless, and she had a nurturing personality. You could tell by the look in Milton's eyes that Hilda was the perfect wife for him. A year later, Milton became the proud father of a son and an ordained minister. We saw him and his family occasionally when we participated in church fundraising and community activities. Every time we saw him he was smiling, and his casual yet slightly dressy attire gave him an appealing look I had never noticed before. His shoes were polished, his clothing was lightly starched and ironed, and his crew haircut, scruffy hotshot beard, and mustache were professionally done. Milton and Daddy's friendship was always solid as a rock. They trusted each other and felt comfortable exchanging their thoughts and ideas to each other. Their friendship was a true connection, and it lasted throughout Daddy's lifetime. It's amazing what love will do for an individual. Love heals our perception of ourselves, touches our hearts, inspires us to be our best selves, helps our bodies fight illnesses, and brings beneficial changes to our immune system. Love is so powerful and important. It helps fight every negative feeling that shouldn't exist in our lives. "Owe no man anything, but to love one another: for he that loveth another hath fulfilled the law" (Rom 13:8).

14

Jesus's Birthday Celebration

Celebrating Christmas was planned throughout the year to make it exciting and joyous, with a focus on the birth of Jesus Christ. Daddy said that when Jesus was born, people came from faraway places to bring gifts and to worship Jesus. He said three wise men gave baby Jesus gold, frankincense, and myrrh. He excitedly read Matt 2:1, 11: "Now when Jesus was born in Bethlehem of Judaea in the days of Herod the king, behold, there came wise men from the east to Jerusalem, . . . And when they were come into the house, they saw the young child with Mary his mother, and fell down, and worshipped him: and when they had opened their treasures, they presented unto him gifts; gold, and frankincense, and myrrh."

Then he said, "Gifts giving is a way to show our love to our Savior and to each other. It reminds me of how joyful people were about having Jesus as our Savior."

Daddy drove us around the Burlington neighborhood at night to see homes and stores decorated. I was amazed at the beautiful decorations and multicolored Christmas trees lit up in the windows. Yard trees, chimneys, porches, bushes, stores, mailboxes, inflatables, and nativity scenes were also lit up. All our Christmas tree decorations were homemade and stitched with colorful yarns. We popped popcorn weeks in advance and cut out colorful paper ornaments for the tree. Mama would dye the popcorn with different colors, and I would help Daddy string the popcorn on tobacco strings to wrap around the Christmas tree. Wrapping the tree was exciting until I couldn't reach the top. Daddy would pick me up to reach the top of the tree, holding me tightly to prevent me from falling. Each Christmas, I would get a kaleidoscope, Life Savers, paper dolls and clothing, a dress, a pair of socks, a pair of shoes, and a brown paper bag of nuts, fruits, and candy. On Christmas day, Daddy would crack open the pecans, Brazil nuts, and hazelnuts with a hammer on the kitchen floor. My job was to throw the shells in the trash can and sweep the floor when he finished. Mama wrapped the Christmas gifts with colorful paper and homemade ribbons, and Daddy wrote my name on each of my Christmas gifts. He arranged the boxes neatly under our "Charlie Brown Christmas tree" and filled my homemade Christmas stocking with a pencil, an eraser, a miniature pencil sharpener, bubble gum, a miniature plastic doll, and a jacks game. Daddy always turned on the Christmas tree lights and Mama served hot apple cider and cookies soon after the tree was lit. The smell of hot apple cider, cakes, cookies, and homemade candies filled the house. I enjoyed his made-up Christmas stories each year and the outcome of each story. His stories were always about a miracle that happened to a family in a small town. Each miracle was different, but the message was the same. The message was to be joyful in giving on Christmas and every day. After reading Christmas stories, Daddy sang the same hymn each year, which was in a song collection book by American clergyman and hymnodist John Henry Hopkins Jr.: "We Three Kings of Orient Are." I sat on the floor in the living room next to his feet, listening to him play the song on his favorite harmonica. The beautiful harmonica music gave me goosebumps. The highlight of Christmas for me was making Christmas gifts for Daddy, Mama, and other family members. Mama taught me how to sew on her sewing machine at an early age. My expert skills were used to make a bright multicolor scarf for Mama, a white handkerchief for Daddy for his "church suit," and painted green, red, orange, and blue tin cans for family members to use for pencil holders or flower vases. At the age of ten, I could sew from a Simplicity Pattern a straight A-line dress or skirt, hem, take out stitches with a seam ripper, lay out pattern pieces on the fabric in the right direction, secure the pattern pieces to the fabric with pins, and cut into the fabric to make a garment. Mama's scarf and Daddy's handkerchief were made from a homemade pattern I had drawn on newspapers. Daddy and Mama were always amazed at my "perfect," straight stitches and how neatly the scarf and handkerchief were ironed. Painting the tin cans was easy to do, but making a design on the painted cans was difficult. I couldn't draw. Even though I didn't have the technique and style, I had confidence that I could create pretty designs on the painted cans with fingernail polish. The outcome was a success! My family loved the floral-designed cans.

Each Christmas, I left milk and cookies for Santa Claus and a letter promising him I had been good. Mama gave me permission to use her homemade red and white tablecloth on the kitchen table. Carefully, I arranged his snacks in Mama's holiday serving dish with a glass of milk and a red cloth napkin. When I saw Santa Claus during the holidays in retail stores, I promised him his snacks would be waiting for him when he came to deliver presents. His eyes lit up with excitement. I was pleased every year that he left me a thank you note for the milk and cookies. I remember one year as a child, I was very upset when I caught Daddy eating and drinking Santa Claus's snacks. It was the only time I was disappointed in him, and I was brave enough to tell him how I felt.

"Why are you eating Santa's cookies and drinking his milk? I promised him I would have cookies and milk waiting for him."

"I'm sorry, Edna. I was hungry. Your mama made plenty of cookies, and we have half a gallon of milk left in the refrigerator. I'm going to put more cookies in the dish and pour another glass of milk before Santa brings your gifts."

"Okay, Daddy. Are you still hungry?"

"No, I'm not hungry."

"If you get hungry again before Santa comes, don't take his snacks on the table. Get your cookies from the cookie jar and your milk from the refrigerator. Then you won't have to worry about putting them back on the table."

"That's a good idea, Edna. I should've thought of doing that myself."

"Let me get another dish and glass. Santa can tell you've been eating out of this dish and drinking out of this glass."

"You're right. Thank you."

I didn't go back to bed until Daddy had filled the dish with cookies and filled the glass with milk. Mama tucked me back into bed after I repeated my prayer again. I could tell Mama had eaten some cookies too, because she had cookie crumbs on her mouth. I didn't need to say anything to Mama because she always ate with Daddy. Whatever Daddy ate, she ate. Daddy listened to me and never ate Santa's snacks again.

Christmas carols were sung on the radio all day, and the singers' voices were beautiful and heartwarming. Everyone that came to our home had the Christmas spirit. They were relatives and longtime friends of Daddy's and

Mama's. Smiles were contagious, hugs were plentiful, and joyful noises were heard throughout the house. They brought gifts, food, nuts, fruits, candy, pies, and fruitcakes for us to enjoy. On Christmas Day, Daddy and Mama waited until the visitors were gone and I was in bed before they gave each other their gifts. Every year the day after Christmas, Mama had on a new pair of earrings and Daddy had on a new shirt. Mama's earrings were always colored stones on silver, and Daddy's shirts were white or pastel blue. Because Mama had no extra money to purchase Christmas gifts, Daddy would give her money to buy his present. Mama wrapped Daddy's shirt in a decorative box she had designed with homemade ribbons, peppermint sticks, pine needles, and holly. It was the prettiest box under the tree. It was a cheerful time in our warm and loving home. I wished Christmas and gift giving was every day. Seeing family and friends happy gave me magical emotions of excitement and joy. True stories prove that miracles do happen at Christmas. Jesus's birth was the greatest miracle of all. Hallelujah!

Christmas wasn't Christmas without a snowman if it snowed during the holidays. With the help of Daddy and Mama, I would roll up three snowballs—one large, one medium, and one small. We stacked them up with the biggest on the bottom, medium in the middle, and the smallest on top for the head. Daddy and Mama let me use my creative mind to make a face, arms, and other accessories. I used a carrot in the middle of his head for his nose, charcoal for his mouth and eyes, and two sticks for his arms. I put Daddy's straw hat on his head and Daddy's black tie around his neck. He was always a fat snowman. After receiving praise from Daddy and Mama for a job well done, Daddy shoveled snow from areas where there was no traffic into two water buckets for Mama to make snow ice cream.

Today, Christmas is important in my household, and I celebrate with my children and extended family with gifts, decorations, Christmas trees, cookies, cakes, pies, nuts, fruit, candy, stockings, holiday songs, Daddy's Bible verses, and Christmas dinner, and I buy myself colored stone earrings on silver. I give no matter how little I have and I love giving so much more than receiving. I built snowmen with my sons during the snowy winter days when they were children, but I wasn't successful at making snow ice cream like Mama. I didn't have her recipe and I couldn't reinvent it. Several Christmases ago, my son Daryl and his wife, Fanchon, gave me a hand-crafted oak kaleidoscope on an oak stand in memory of Daddy. It was the greatest and most meaningful gift ever!

15

Fear Not

Daddy protected me when I was scared, but he taught me to lean on God because he and Mama wouldn't be with me all the time.

"God is the only one who will be with you and never leave you."

Unlike other children in my neighborhood, I wasn't afraid of snakes, creepy crawling insects, dogs, and elevators, but I was scared out of my mind of the dark, thunder, and lightning. I thanked God for Daddy and Mama easing my anxieties with compassion. At nighttime, Daddy wouldn't leave my bedroom light on because he wanted to "reduce the electricity bill." I couldn't sleep at night, so Daddy compromised and lit a candle to burn all night. Before leaving my room, he smiled and said, "Edna, you're going to be alright." Always after Daddy left my room, Mama would come in and kiss me good night, straighten out my bedspread, and give me the biggest, most caring hug. We had plenty of large homemade candles in mason jars throughout the house. Mama made the candle with wax, a wick, and sticks for support. She would melt the wax in a pot on the stove, pour the wax into the large mason jar, and place the wick in the middle of the melted wax. She would use sticks to keep the wick in place and make sure it didn't slide in the melted wax. Once the no-fragrance wax had cooled, mama would trim the wick down and distribute candles to all the rooms in the house for emergency use. Being afraid of the dark was my emergency, and Daddy tried in so many ways to help me end my fear of darkness, including explaining the purpose of it.

"If the world was light all day and night, you wouldn't be able to sleep and your body will slowly stop working. You would get tired and weak, not be able to think, look old, get sick, and gradually die. You can't live without sleep. Darkness is a gift from God. Darkness is necessary for you to give your body rest, which will give you energy to walk, talk, play with your friends, help your mama in the house, and make good grades in school. Everything and everyone God created is good, including you. You're special in his eyes and my eyes too."

"Thank you, Daddy. I love you."

"I love you too."

Daddy did a good job explaining why darkness was essential for sleeping, but his explanation didn't work. One Friday after school, Daddy told me I was going to stay at the house of Miss Nancy, a neighbor and close friend of the family. Daddy and Mama had to go to a funeral out of town on Saturday, and they wouldn't be back until the next Sunday.

"Your mama has already taken your clothes over to Nancy. I gave your mama a brown bag to give to Nancy with a note inside of it to read to make sure you will be alright. Don't forget to say your prayers before going to bed and be helpful to her. She is so excited you are going to spend the week with her."

Not a word came from my mouth, but I gave a pursed smile. I wasn't excited about staying with Miss Nancy because she didn't have any children, and I had never seen any lights on at her house at night. She was frugal and grew all her vegetables and fruits for canning and drying to eat throughout the winter months. She had huge apple trees, pear trees, and strawberry and blackberry patches that neighbors helped her harvest to sell in order to supplement her income. She had hogs, chickens, and cows each year to kill for meat. The children in the neighborhood collected eggs and carefully placed them in egg cartons for her. She used them for breakfast and for recipes. She gave fruits and vegetables instead of money to pay those who helped her. Her clothes were old but clean, and her shoes were worn but polished. She didn't throw away anything, including leftovers, and she didn't ask for anything. If she saw a penny on the ground, she would pick it up and put it in her pocket.

"Pennies makes nickels, nickels make dimes, dimes make quarters, quarters make fifty cents, and fifty cents make dollars."

She quoted the penny approach every time she found a penny. If she found a nickel, dime, quarter, or fifty-cent piece, she didn't say anything.

Sometimes she would walk to the local store just to look for coins on the ground. She never purchased anything when I was with her.

I voiced my concern to Daddy and Mama. "I know she's not going to leave the light on because she doesn't want the electric bill to go up."

Voicing my concern was a waste of time because it didn't change Daddy's plan. I had to spend a week with Miss Nancy. Entertainment that first night was listening to Bible stories and drawing pictures of animals when she named them. Every time I drew an animal, she would give me a big, warm hug and praise my pitiful drawing. I had no natural talent in drawing like Daddy did, and I didn't have a desire to put time and effort into learning. She was so nice and kind to me. I felt so secure in her home that I had almost forgotten about the dark bedroom I had to sleep in.

"Edna, I'm going to get your room ready for bed. I will be right back to get you. Keep drawing."

My body started shivering, and I could feel my heart beat faster. I had to find courage to tell her I was afraid. I closed my eyes and prayed silently.

"Oh God, please tell me what to say to Miss Nancy. I know it's not polite to tell her what to do in her house, but I'm afraid."

Miss Nancy scared me when she tapped me on the back of my shoulder. She smiled and took me by my left hand and guided me down the hallway.

"Your bedroom is ready, Edna. You will be in the bedroom next to mine in case you need me in the middle of the night. I put an extra blanket at the foot of your bed for you to use if you need it. Sometimes it gets a little chilly at night."

Miss Nancy had no idea how much I was going to need her, and it wasn't going to be in the middle of the night. I was going to need her as soon as she turned the light off. I was upset because God hadn't told me what to say to her, and it was hard for me to wait on God. I had to come up with something quick to make her keep the light on.

"Thank you."

Suddenly I had an overwhelming fear as I got closer to the bedroom door. My legs became weak and I felt like I was going to faint. Miss Nancy couldn't see me because she walked in front of me. She opened the door and pointed for me to go in. Hesitantly, I slowly walked into the bedroom. I was shocked and relieved to see a big candle lit on the nightstand next to my bed. It was identical to the candles mama made.

"You have a candle, just like the ones we have at home!" I said.

"Your Daddy sent this candle, a match pack, and a note in a separate bag by your mama when she brought your clothes over. He made sure I didn't miss seeing it."

"What did the note say?"

She pulled the note out of her pocket and began reading. "It says, 'Edna sleeps every night with a lit candle. I will be grateful if you light this candle every night for her. It will remind her of being home and she will rest better. Thank you, Nancy, for taking care of Edna for us. We will be back home next Sunday.'"

"He made sure his little girl felt at home. What a sweet daddy you have."

Daddy had taken care of me again, and I loved him for coming to my rescue without me knowing. He knew I would be afraid of sleeping in the dark, but he didn't tell Miss Nancy. He saved me from being embarrassed about exposing my inner fear to a person I didn't feel comfortable telling it to.

"I have a super, super good daddy."

I had a wonderful week with Miss Nancy because of Daddy, but no home made me feel at ease like our home. Our home was where I felt safe to have hope, dreams, fears, and freedom to be myself.

I was overjoyed the minute I saw Daddy and Mama walk into Miss Nancy's house to pick me up.

"Thank you, Miss Nancy, for keeping me. I had a good time."

"I enjoyed you being here. Come back to see me again."

"Okay. Bye, Miss Nancy."

"Bye, darling."

That night I promised Daddy I would never get angry at God again. What Daddy said to me at the end of our discussion has given me peace and patience to this day while waiting on God to answer my prayers.

"Be still and wait on God. God may not come when you want him to, but he will come right on time."

Daddy's words were similar to Ps 37:7: "Rest in the LORD, and wait patiently for him: fret not thyself because of him who prospereth in his way, because of the man who bringeth wicked devices to pass."

Being patient is still difficult, especially when I'm anxious. Thunder and lightning were the most terrifying experience I ever encountered as a child. When I heard a loud booming sound from thunder and saw the crackling flash of light from lightning, I would scrawl under my bed. I was afraid to scream, but I was crying hysterically and waiting for Daddy and Mama to come to my room. Daddy and Mama always turned the television off and didn't say one word during the storm. No one was allowed to talk during the storm. Daddy would kneel down and pull me out from under the bed. He would pick me up, carry me to the living room, and sit me on Mama's lap. Together, we waited quietly for the storm to end. During the wait, I buried my face on Mama's chest and cried silently. Mama wrapped her arms around me to calm me down and stop my shaking, and she whispered a prayer that I barely heard: "Calm her . . . in the name of Jesus, Amen."

Daddy had an explanation for why we needed to be silent: "God is angry and we need to let him do his work."

One morning after a severe storm, I joined Daddy and Mama at the breakfast table. I could tell by Daddy's and Mama's faces that they were concerned about something. I didn't dare ask what was wrong because I knew it was about me. Daddy's "good morning" sounded exhausted, and dark circles were under his eyes. Mama's eyes were puffy and her face showed tiredness. She opened up the topic of discussion as she passed the eggs, country ham, and biscuits around the table.

"Edna, we need to talk about the way you acted last night when it thundered and lightninged. Your daddy and I are worried that you could harm yourself. Last night you knocked over the lit candle in your bedroom trying to escape the storm. You could have caught the house on fire and killed all of us. We didn't rest well last night because we were afraid you might need us in the middle of the night during the storm. Don't think I'm trying to make you feel bad—I'm trying to help you. I understand how you feel because I get scared sometimes too, but we have to trust in God. We're going to work through this together."

I didn't say anything because every word Mama said was the truth, and I had no comeback for my erratic behavior. I could tell by the expression on Daddy's face that he was concerned and eager to talk with me. I kept eating and didn't look up because I was embarrassed beyond comprehension. Just like Mama, Daddy spoke nicely and clearly.

"If you trust in God and pray, you won't be afraid. God is good, and he loves you. He is the light of the world. He will protect you from the thunder and storms, and he is your light when it's dark. His light is brighter than the sun, and his light will shine on you all the time if you have faith in him.

Once you have faith and trust him, nothing will frighten you and you will rest in peace. Now let's pray."

Mama, Daddy, and I closed our eyes, holding each other's hands in a circle. While Daddy was praying, I was thinking about a plan to hide my fear and prevent me from screaming again. I didn't want Daddy and Mama to think I didn't trust in God, but trusting God didn't take away my fears. Every night for weeks, I read Isa 41:13–14: "For I the Lord thy God will hold thy right hand, saying unto thee, Fear not; I will help thee. Fear not, thou worm Jacob, and ye men of Israel; I will help thee, saith the Lord, and thy redeemer, the Holy One of Israel." Because the Bible said so, I knew I could depend on God. There were many more years of storms, lights burned out, candles lit, tears, and screaming. Nothing changed except that Mama added fragrance to every candle to give our house a scent of honeysuckle, and during holidays the scent of apple and cinnamon. Daddy and Mama continued reminding me of God's love, and we prayed together, giving God thanks for keeping us safe through the storms. They never made me feel ashamed of my actions, and they never made me feel unloved. After every storm or candle burned out during the night, they promised me that God was with me through it all. Now when it's lightning or thundering, I don't scream, cry, or crawl under my bed but stay silent so "God can do his work." A night-light is on every night when I go to sleep, and I have extras on hand if I need them. I ask God to protect me and my loved ones every night before closing my eyes. Each morning, I thank God for waking me up. He didn't have to do it, but he did. During the day and through the night, it's God who keeps my heart beating. God is the ultimate healer of all time!

16

Farm Work Isn't for Me

Work ethic was introduced to me at an early age during some of the summers on the family farm. The memories of getting up at the crack of dawn, plowing the fields, having sweat all over my body from the hot weather, sucking tobacco, having hands blackened by sticky tobacco tar, handing tobacco leaves to the tobacco stringer, and sometimes tying tobacco, made me appreciate the jobs I had in my later years. When we weren't in the fields, we were collecting eggs, digging potatoes from the ground, pulling corn and tomatoes from their vines, milking the cows, churning milk, canning fruits and vegetables, picking up apples that had fallen from the apple tree, and sorting through the apples to make sure there were no insects or signs of disease. The hard work brought me to exhaustion, but it was necessary for my uncles and aunts to complete the process in a timely manner for sale. It supplemented their income and provided food for all of us.

In spite of the necessity, I thought of every trick in the book to get out of going to the farm, but it didn't work.

The second summer I was scheduled to work on the farm, I made up several excuses one after the other to avoid going.

"My head is hurting . . ."

"I didn't sleep good last night . . ."

"My stomach hurts . . "

"A snake almost bit me . . ."

"My feet were sore and I could hardly walk . . ."

"I almost fainted in the field . . ."

"I'm afraid of the cows . . ."

"The horse almost stepped on my feet . . ."

Daddy had heard enough of me complaining and he wasn't going to hear any more excuses.

"Edna, you asked to go help every summer. Nobody made you go. Now if you don't like working on the farm, just say it, because making up all these stories isn't right. What does the Bible say about lying?"

"I don't remember."

"'Lying lips are abomination to the Lord: but they that deal truly are his delight,' Proverbs 12:22. Do you remember me reading this verse to you?"

"Yes sir."

"We're going to talk about this verse some more. After I talk to you, you can stay or go. It's up to you."

"Yes sir."

"You are young now and you don't have to worry about bills, a house to live in, food, car payments, or work. It is my responsibility to make sure you are taken care of and your mama helps by making money sewing and cooking for all of us. Now a dollar bill can buy you a hot dog, soda pop, french fries, and ice cream. There's going to come a time when a dollar won't even buy you a hot dog. When you're old enough, you will get married and will have to help your husband pay the bills. The only way you can help is by working. Money is not going to fall out of the sky—you have to earn it. He won't be able to do it by himself unless he's rich. Even if he's rich, you will have to help him by working in your home. Money earned is the only way to survive. If you try to steal it, you will get locked up or killed. If you beg for it, people will get tired of giving you money when you are able to work. If you become bitter because you were too lazy to work, your family and friends will stay away from you. Most importantly, it's a sin. When we sin, we separate ourselves from God."

"Daddy, you said God will provide."

"Yes, he will provide by giving you work to do. The good book says, 'He that tilleth his land shall be satisfied with bread: but he that followeth vain persons is void of understanding,' Proverbs 12:11. In the good book, there are many verses about working: Colossians 3:23–24; Ephesians 4:28; John 6:27; Galatians 6:4–5; Psalm 90:7; Proverbs 6:10–12; 12:24; 13:4; 16:3;

Phillippians 4:13; Genesis 2:3, 15; Luke 1:37; 1 Timothy 2:6; 5:8; Jeremiah 29:11; and Titus 2:7–8.

"Wow, that's a lot!"

"You're right. Now that you know God wants us to work, I need to tell you the right way to go about it."

"Okay."

"When you take a job, you have to come to work every day as you promised until the job is completed and be respectful. Don't play around while working, don't talk bad about your supervisor, and do what your supervisor asks you to do. Your supervisor wants to be able to trust and depend on you."

"Even if the supervisor is my uncle?"

"It doesn't matter if your supervisor is a family member or a stranger—God wants you to be a good worker. Supervisors don't have time to watch over their help all day and they don't have time to tell their help over and over again what need to be done. A good helper makes it easy for their supervisors and other helpers. The worst thing a helper can do is not show up for work. Do you know why?"

"No sir."

"Because when a helper doesn't show up, the work doesn't get done. When the work doesn't get done, the supervisor won't get paid. Nobody is going to pay a supervisor because he got part of the job done. Supervisors have bosses too. Their bosses have to make money too, and if they're not satisfied with the work, they will go somewhere else. One helper not showing up can change a lot of lives for the worse. Do you know what happens when the supervisor doesn't get paid?"

"He can't buy anything for his children."

"Yes, you're right. His helpers will suffer too. The helpers who worked so hard won't have any money either. Their families will be hungry. They will live on the street because they won't have money to pay for their homes and their cars, and they can become sick because of worrying.

Let's pretend you have a lemonade stand and you asked three friends to help you sell lemonade. You're the supervisor. One of your friends worked hard and asked everyone that passed by if they wanted to buy lemonade. The second friend just stood by and watched, and the third friend that promised to come didn't show up. Because one friend didn't help and the other one didn't show up, you and your friend couldn't pour the lemonade fast enough. Over half of your customers left because they were tired of waiting in the hot sun in the long line. You didn't make enough money to pay for renting the lemonade stand, to pay back the money you borrowed to buy lemons and cups, and to pay your friend who worked very hard. Even though the other friend stood and watched, you have to pay her too because she was on the job. How do you feel about this, Miss Supervisor? How are you going to pay two helpers and the person you borrowed the money from? How can you help your friend, who can't buy medicine for her mother?"

My head was spinning around because I didn't know how to deal with the situation. Feeling down and helpless, tears came down my face because I didn't have an answer. Also, the thought of someone not being able to get medicine because of me was heartbreaking.

"Daddy, I don't think I should have to pay my friend for standing around and not helping."

"No, you don't have to pay her if you told her you didn't need her to do the job. If you didn't tell her, you have to pay her. It's your job as a supervisor to train her and decide if she can do the job. Let's pretend you didn't tell her. Now the friend that didn't come to work will not get paid. Is there anything you can do?"

"There isn't anything I can do to pay my two friends or the person I borrowed the money from. The only thing I can do with the little money I made is to buy medicine for my friend's mother."

"There isn't anything you can do to make this situation better, but there are things you can do to make money for the next lemonade stand sale. You can make your own lemonade stand, save money to buy your lemons and cups, and make sure that when you ask someone to help, you can depend on them. How do you feel about the helper that didn't show up?"

"She didn't tell me the truth, and I will never trust her again."

"What would you have done differently if you knew she wasn't going to work?"

"I would get my other friend to help me."

"Great answer. What if your friend apologized for not showing up? Would you get her to help you with your next lemonade stand sale?"

"No."

"Why?"

"Because I wouldn't believe anything she said. The helpers have to get paid. She didn't care about anybody but herself."

"Your uncle and aunt will feel the same way about you if you didn't show up."

Daddy was brilliant in how he got his point across to me calmly and effectively. He gave good examples and reasoning without being condescending. He never talked down to me, and I felt like I was on equal footing. He maintained an even keel and spoke clearly and gently to me. Never during his teaching did I feel intimidated. His examples were captivating and productive, and they brought out a true picture of what could happen if I didn't help my uncle and aunt. His stories were always attention grabbers, but brief and concise. Quickly I understood that on a job it is important to maintain good attendance, display a positive and respectful attitude toward my bosses and coworkers, perform my job according to a reasonable, acceptable standard, conduct myself in a professional manner, and follow procedures when dealing with problems or issues.

"Daddy, what if I don't like the job? Do I have to go next summer?"

"No, but you have to tell them so they can get someone to take your place. Remember, you said if you had known your friend wasn't going to show up, you would have gotten your other friend to help."

"Yes sir."

"Your uncle and aunt need to know so they will have plenty of time to get someone to take your place."

"Do I tell them when I get there or when I leave?"

"I don't know if there is a right time to tell them, but I think you should tell them when you leave. Don't tell them in front of the other helpers. You don't want them knowing your business."

"What do I say to them?"

"Tell them you won't be back next summer."

"What if they ask me why?"

"Why don't you want to come back?"

"Because I have to get up early, it's too hot, I don't like that black sticky stuff on my hands, I'm scared of those worms, I have to work so hard, and I get tired, Daddy. I hate working in tobacco."

"Well, you have lots of reasons you don't want to go back. Don't say you hate the job. If they ask you why, say you won't be coming back next summer because the sun makes you sick. Make sure you wear white or light-colored clothing to cover yourself while working in the field. White or light-colored clothing keeps you from getting a lot of heat."

"Okay, Daddy."

That summer was the best summer working on the farm because I knew I didn't have to come back again. Also, I didn't want to be the reason for my coworkers' unemployment, homelessness, hunger, and lack of medicine for their sick ones. I did any chores that needed to be done without being told to, including helping with breakfast at five o'clock every morning. After eating breakfast, I was the first one on the back of the truck to ride to the barn where the tobacco was waiting on the uneven, long wooden table to be strung.

Since it was my last summer working—and having nothing to lose—I was bold enough to ask the older helpers if I could tie tobacco. They never asked me what I would like to do, but they had no problem telling me what to do. There was no fun in handing leaves to the tobacco stringer because it was relatively easy and mindless work. Tying tobacco was challenging and required skills, focus, and the art of tying the bundles tightly and evenly onto the sticks. Also, the barn was built to hold up to five hundred tobacco sticks to successfully cure the tobacco. It was necessary to keep count of the number of sticks tied to prevent waste. Checking the sticks before tying the tobacco to make sure the sticks were strong enough to hold the tobacco made me feel more valued. If I didn't feel the sticks were strong enough to hang in the barn on tier poles, I was allowed to make the decision to throw the stick away. When I made the decision that a stick wouldn't hold the weight, the helpers threw the stick away without arguing or disrespecting. Their calm personalities and helpfulness made my job smooth and successful. My duties as a tobacco stringer included supervising the farm workers. I helped them save time by checking the tobacco sticks beforehand to prevent them redoing work because of tobacco falling off a broken stick. We saved a lot of time, and they showed their appreciation by giving me hugs at the end of the day. They needed someone to learn from and thrive with, and I learned from them to never assume, to communicate effectively, and to work intently.

The best outcome of leading the farm helpers was that I had positive memories to take back home with me, and I discovered how much I enjoyed bringing the best performance out of people. Before I left to work on the farm my last summer, Daddy prayed for me and read a verse from the Bible: "Whatsoever thy hand findeth to do, do it with thy might; for there is no work, nor device, nor knowledge, nor wisdom, in the grave, whither thou goest" (Eccl 9:10). When I waved goodbye to my friends, Daddy's prayer and verse from Ecclesiastes came to my mind. My heart was so full of joy knowing that working can be fun if you keep God in it. It was a valuable lesson I carried with me throughout my working career.

My job performance and positive attitude were praised by Uncle Joe and Aunt Lucille. One Sunday night after I had turned off the light switch to go to sleep, Aunt Lucille knocked on my bedroom door and cracked the door open.

"Edna, is it okay if I come in?"

"Yes ma'am."

She kissed me on the cheek, sat next to me, and smiled.

"Tomorrow morning you will be going home, and I wanted to talk to you alone. Joe and I are going to miss you."

"I'm going to miss you too."

"Joe and I were talking about what a wonderful job you did on the farm and in the house. You have helped me so much around the house: churning buttermilk, cooking, washing and drying dishes, and helping me serve the helpers on the farm. You have been an angel to check the chicken coop for eggs every evening after a hard day's work. I'm going to tell Herbert and Willie how smart and sweet you are. I know they're proud of you."

"Thank you."

"Joe is proud of you too. He said he has never seen you tie tobacco so fast and tight on the sticks. You really surprised him. He said not one leaf fell off. He said the other helpers couldn't keep up with you."

"They let me tie tobacco instead of handing leaves."

"You don't like handing leaves?"

"Oh yes, I like handing leaves, but I like tying tobacco better."

"Oh, I see. So from now on, that will be your job during the summer."

I had knots in my stomach because it was time to tell her I wasn't coming back. No matter how much fun I'd had leading the older helpers and problem-solving, tobacco farming wasn't what I wanted to do for a career.

"Well, uh, uh, uh."

Holding my head down didn't cover up my stress or the fact that I was overwhelmed with emotions. Aunt Lucille knew something was wrong. It was excruciating to tell her I wouldn't be back another summer after she had praised my work performance, but I had to do it to give her time to find someone else to work in my place.

"Edna, are you alright? You're trembling."

"Well, I'm a little upset."

"Why?"

Because I have to tell you something."

"What is it, sweetie?"

"This is my last summer working. I won't be back."

Aunt Lucille leaned over next to me and put her arms around me.

"Sweetie, it's okay. You don't have to be afraid to tell me you're not coming back. Joe and I are thankful for how much you have helped us during the summers. You deserve to enjoy your summers with your friends."

"Really?"

"Of course! We're going to miss you on the farm during the summer, but we will see you when we visit your daddy and mama, and when they visit us. That's the good thing about family. Don't you worry one minute about not coming back. We will be alright. Thank you for letting me know in time to find someone else. You're a good worker."

"Thank you."

"Now I need to finish what I came in here to do. Joe and I decided we're going to give you some extra money because you worked so hard."

Aunt Lucille reached into her dress pocket and pulled out a tied-up handkerchief.

"Untie it and see what's in it."

When I saw the money in the handkerchief, my hands began trembling and I almost dropped it. There was enough money in the handkerchief to buy all my school clothes and shoes for the school year.

"Oh my goodness! Thank y'all so much."

"You deserve it. Don't tell a soul but your daddy and mama."

"I won't tell anybody!"

It was the best day of my life, and it was a relief not having to explain to Uncle Joe and Aunt Lucille why I was leaving. My hard work paid off and I owed it all to Daddy. That summer, he taught me in one discussion why a good work ethic is necessary to my employer and to myself. Because of Daddy, I viewed work from a different perspective. I performed my duties with positive moral values that included integrity, responsibility, dependability, high quality, discipline, humility, and teamwork. Working is healthy, but the quality of my work makes an immense difference.

Throughout my life in my leadership positions, my main focus was to make sure the employees I managed had job security to take care of their families. If an employee was having difficulty performing his job responsibilities, I gave him plenty of time and tools to improve his work performance. I made sure the employee had a solid understanding of the responsibilities of his job, and I provided ongoing coaching. Feedback was given on what needed to be improved. If things got egregious, I would place the worker in another position where they could succeed. Thank God I had plenty of different positions to transfer an employee to. The thought of an employee losing a job and not being able to care for his family crushed me. My method created a win-win situation: continued employment for the employee and the maintaining of my team's credibility.

17

Church Folks

When Daddy was upset about something he couldn't control or he couldn't figure out a good solution, he would walk back and forth across the backyard, regardless of the weather. One sunny autumn evening after we arrived home from church, Daddy didn't go into the house with Mama. He didn't talk at all on the way home, and Mama didn't pressure him for conversation. Something must have happened when he was talking with a group of men before leaving church. He walked to the backyard, took off his suit jacket, and laid it carefully on the porch step. He began walking at a fast pace. Trying to keep up with him wasn't easy because I had to run to stay beside him.

"What's wrong, Daddy?"

"Nothing."

"Then why are you walking so fast?"

"Just go in the house."

"Do I have to?"

"Yes, you do."

I stopped, got my breath back, and turned to go into the house.

"Wait a minute, Edna. I need to talk to you about what happened to-day in church. I don't want you growing up being like those ignorant people who call themselves Christians. Let's go in the house so your mama can hear it too."

Mama was in the kitchen warming up our Sunday dinner and listen-ing to gospel music on the radio.

"Let's help your mama get the food on the table, and we will talk while we're eating."

I set the table, Daddy took the food to the table, and Mama turned the radio off and poured lemonade into each glass. Daddy had our undivided attention during his heartfelt conversation.

"Did either one of you notice anything different in church today?"

Mama and I said no simultaneously.

"I'm glad to hear you didn't notice anything out of the ordinary. The only thing we should be noticing in church are God's words. Unfortunately, several people did, and you won't believe what they said about it. I'm beginning to question if we need to go to church somewhere else."

Daddy's deep voice was powerful, empathetic, and genuine. He very seldom called a family meeting, and when he did, Mama and I wouldn't say a word while he was talking. We knew that when he felt strongly about something, it was best not to say anything because he was going to get his point across no matter what.

"We had a nice couple visit our church today. They were friendly and eager to fellowship with the congregation, and I thought we would be the same way. Unlike others, they sat in the front row to make sure they heard the sermon. Just like everyone else in church, they celebrated their faith in God through worshiping, singing gospel songs with the choir, and praying with the congregation. They were there because it was the right thing to do to honor God's day. They could have visited any church, but they chose our church. We all need each other to lean on to make it through tough times. The church is needed to help us keep our faith through preaching and teaching. It's the only place we can worship peacefully and speak freely of our great God without persecution. The church is God's house, and hospitality should be given to everyone. I was embarrassed at how our members wouldn't slide down the pews to make room for the couple to sit down. After church, the couple introduced themselves to everyone they met, but a lot of our church members walked away. Do you know why they walked away?"

Again, Mama and I said no simultaneously.

"They walked away from them because they were from another country and they were dressed differently. Some of the men met after church to talk about what they didn't like about the couple. They should've been talking about how to make them feel welcomed and a part of our congregation. One of the deacons had the nerve to say they were bad people just because they're not Americans, and the other men agreed. They were cowards and didn't stand up for what is right. They're going to burst hell wide open if they don't change. They said they didn't want them back at our church because they believed in evil spirits. I couldn't believe I heard those words coming from the mouths of members of our church who call themselves Christians. They had never seen the couple before today, but they're telling lies on them. They have embarrassed me. Lord have mercy on their souls! I told them they were wrong and that if it took the last breath in me, I wouldn't let them stop the couple from coming to church. They were mad at me, but I don't care. If they go to hell, they're not taking me with them. They're always talking about how people treat them and how they can't get work because of the color of their skin, but they're doing the same thing. Who gave them the right to treat people like nobody? Everybody is somebody! I'm calling Reverend Thomas as soon as I finish dinner. They're stupid! Can't do nothing with a stupid man."

Mama was shaking her head with disappointment, but I could tell by her body movement that she knew who Daddy was talking about. I was racking my brain trying to figure out who the couple was in church, but I wasn't successful. The church was crowded and I wasn't tall enough to look everyone in the eye, and I didn't look up unless someone spoke to me. Mama was friendly but quiet, and she didn't spend time mingling with the ladies after church. After church, she spoke to everyone she passed by, but she and I went directly to the car and waited for Daddy. On our way out of church that day, the only thing I had noticed was a lady wearing a beautiful, colorful purple and orange silk dress that was long and wrapped, a purple and orange silk scarf across her shoulders, and hand-painted purple moccasins with feathers. Her hair was jet black and and was pulled back into a low, braided bun. The man with her was wearing an embroidered, white silk coat with purple buttons, white silk trousers, purple headdress, and tan moccasins. Their brown skin tone wasn't as dark as that of some of the church members, but they were more beautiful in appearance than most of the congregation. The man didn't take his headgear off during the sermon, but the men who were members didn't take off their Sunday hats either. I concluded they were husband and wife because they were wearing rings with matching stones on their left ring fingers. If the congregation was talking about them, they had to be jealous of them to treat them that way. The couple didn't look like they believed in evil spirits, and they didn't bother anybody. They spoke to us with smiles when we were exiting out the church door. He was polite and held the door open for Mama and me.

"Edna, never ever mistreat someone because of where they come from, the color of their skin, how they look, or if they're rich or poor. If you do, you will never get anywhere in life. I have been mistreated by a lot of people because of the color of my skin, because I didn't have the money or worthless things other people had, and because people couldn't tell me what to do. You know what? Only God can tell me what to do. I got my money honestly by working hard. I never wanted to be like anyone else because I don't know what they did to get ahead or who they hurt to get it. I've never been ashamed of the color of my skin because God gave it to me just like he gave different skin colors to everyone else.

"I always thought he gave us different skin colors to test our love for each other and faith in him. A lot of people have failed the test. Pitiful! If everyone had the same color of skin and same eye or hair color, there would be no way of knowing if we have love in our hearts. God is smart. He knows how to test us. You know what I do when people treat me wrong? I pray for them because they sure need it. I want you to do the same. Don't do evil because they do evil. Evilness will destroy your soul. Let God take care of the haters. Don't miss the blessings God has for you. It's stupid to be that way, and you will not get into heaven hating. Love everyone. You'll never know what person will help you when you're sick or hungry. Stand up for what is right and God will bless you. Standing up for what is wrong is the work of the devil. The devil will promise you everything to get you to do evil, but as soon as he is finished using you, he will drop you like a hot potato and destroy you. God never leaves you, and his love is everlasting.

"I'm going to read some verses from the good book. 'Be not forgetful to entertain strangers: for thereby some have entertained angels unawares,' Hebrew 13:2. 'If there be therefore any consolation in Christ, if any comfort of love, if any fellowship of the Spirit, if any bowels and mercies, fulfill ye my joy, that ye be likeminded, having the same love, being of one accord, of one mind. Let nothing be done through strife or vainglory; but in lowliness of mind let each esteem others better than themselves. Look not every man on his own things, but every man also on the things of others,' Philippians 2:1–4."

"Daddy, you said church folks are supposed to bring people to God."

"That is exactly what I said."

"Well, they're not going to bring nobody to God acting like that."

"You're right. The devil is busy and doing a good job keeping people away from what is right. Some of the members are falling into the devil's trap. They're making the church look bad acting like that."

"Daddy, I promise I won't fall into the devil's trap. I'm going to be nice to everybody."

"God will be pleased."

The Sundays following the incident, the congregation acted differently toward the couple and treated them in a loving Christian way. The church folks were attentive to them and went out of their way to make sure they felt comfortable, loved, and valued. The couple was involved in teaching Sunday school, fundraising, and helping with programs and other church activities. Their facial expressions showed they were happy to be members of our church, as well as how appreciative they were of the fellowship. Daddy did something to improve the behavior of the church folks, but he never told me what he said or did to change their attitudes. It didn't matter to me what he did or said. What mattered to me was that Daddy wasn't frustrated anymore and he wasn't leaving our church. I loved our church. Also, it was amazing to see him stand up for righteousness.

I learned at an early age that people shouldn't be judged because of where they come from or the color of their skin, but by the character within. It was the most valuable and rewarding lesson Daddy ever taught me. Embracing diversity is the key to knowledge. I love meeting people with different backgrounds, skills, and experiences. When people of different races, nationalities, sexes, and religions come together, the individual and society benefit, resulting in fresh ideas and perceptions. I can't imagine my life without diversity. I'm a member of a diverse church where the pastor's and congregation's Christian beliefs are obvious by their actions. I feel empty and unfilled when I miss a Sunday worship service. Everyone is welcomed, regardless of their race or what country they come from. We help each other when our faith becomes weak, and we rejoice together over God's goodness and his unconditional love for us. They genuinely love me and I love them, and I'm blessed to have them in my life. My best friends are African Americans, Asians, Whites, Hispanics, and Latinos. We have learned so much from each other, and we support each other through good and bad. I'm an advocate for fairness for all people, regardless of their race or where they come from, and I build people up when they're down and remind them of how special they are.

18

Honor Your Father and Mother

Daddy always purchased his gas on Saturday mornings at a family-owned gas station nearby. After paying for his gas, he would stay in the store until he finished reading the local newspaper. The newspaper was a perk for regular customers to show the store owner's appreciation. Although I had to play in front of the window where Daddy could see me, I played hopscotch every time I came with him to the gas station. Hopscotch was challenging and fun, and I loved to see people stop and watch me. Setting up for the game—drawing squares large enough for one foot—required focus. I drew the hopscotch design on the unpaved ground with a stick, and I made sure the rock thrown into the squares wouldn't bounce out easily. The squares were big enough for my foot, and the rock was heavy enough to stay in the squares. I enjoyed hopping on one foot and balancing myself so I wouldn't fall. I had become a professional at tossing my rock successfully into each square, and I was eager to show off. One Saturday while hopscotching, a little girl and her mother stopped to watch me play. I had never seen the little girl before, but I had seen the woman many times at community fish fries and holiday programs. She was always nice, but she never smiled at anyone. That day she was almost unrecognizable. She was smiling, her face was glowing, and she didn't have a scarf covering her hair. Her hair was beautiful and her skin looked healthier than ever before. It was evident she was enjoying her little girl. The little girl anxiously began pleading with her mother.

"Can I play with her, Mama? Please, please, can I?"

"Well, I think we need to ask her."

The little girl looked me, anxious for an answer.

"You can play with me."

The woman continued the conversation by saying, "My name is Irene Enoch."

"My name is Edna."

Irene looked at the little girl. "Do you want to tell Edna your name?"

"My name is Lynette Enoch. I'm adopted. She's my mama and I have a daddy too."

Mrs. Irene chuckled.

"Lynette tells everybody she meets that she is adopted. Bless her heart."

I smiled, but I didn't say anything because I didn't know the meaning of adoption. Daddy had told me many times not to pretend like I knew something when I didn't. He said people will know you're a fake.

"Do you mind showing Lynette how to play hopscotch? She has never played hopscotch before."

"Yes ma'am, I will show her."

"Thank you, Edna. It will only take me a few minutes to pick up some items and pay for the gas."

"Okay."

"Lynette, please be good so you can play with her again."

"Yes ma'am."

Lynette had a difficult time following instructions, and she didn't waste any time making up her own rules. She threw the stone outside all the squares near the building and left it there. She skipped into all the squares to the end and ran back to the first squares over and over again. She grabbed my hand and I ran with her with little enthusiasm. She was feeling good, almost euphoric. I was feeling miserable and played out. Lynette didn't realize she had ruined the art of hopscotching and no one was interested in watching us. Instead, customers dodged us to keep us from running into them. Nevertheless, Lynette's happiness was more important to me than entertaining the customers. Mrs. Irene trusted me to take care of Lynette for a few minutes, and I wasn't going to let her down. I was almost out of breath when Mrs. Irene came out of the store. She walked over to me and pulled out a big, colorful lollipop from the brown paper bag she was carrying.

"Edna, your daddy said it was okay for me to give you a lollipop."

"Wow! Thank you so much, Mrs Irene."

"Thank you for watching Lynette."

"Mama, can I have a lollipop too?"

"Yes. I will give it to you as soon as we get in the car."

"I don't want to go home! I want to play with her!"

Anxiety began building up in me from the fear of Lynette staying longer to play with me.

"You can play with Edna again."

"Please, can I stay?"

"No, not this time. We have to help Daddy clean the smokehouse."

"Okay."

"Say goodbye to Edna."

"Bye."

Relieved, I waved goodbye to Lynette.

On the way home, Daddy and I engaged in a lengthy conversation about my playtime with Lynette. Eating my lollipop on the way home made my conversation with Daddy more relaxing and enjoyable.

"Edna, did you have fun playing with Lynette?"

"She was a handful. I was so tired of her acting up. I didn't know what to do with her."

"What did she do?"

"She never stopped running. She was supposed to hop. That's why it's called hopscotch. No matter what I said, she wouldn't listen."

Daddy chuckled.

"Taking care of someone is a big job, isn't it?"

"Uh huh, I won't do that again."

"It was nice of Irene to give you a lollipop. She was happy Lynette had someone to play with."

"It's a good lollipop. It tastes like the vanilla and strawberry flavoring mama cooks with."

"I'm glad you like it."

"Daddy, what is adoption?"

"Where did you hear that word from?"

"Lynette said she was adopted."

"Fred and Irene got themselves a lawyer to make Lynette their daughter because they wanted a child. They had to sign papers to make them Lynette's parents by law. You can't go against the law. They're responsible for raising her as their own child, and the real parents can't take her back. It's called adoption."

"Why did Lynette's daddy and mama give her away?"

"I don't know why Lynette was adopted. I do know there are lots of good reasons why parents give their children away."

"What are the good reasons?"

"Sometimes, parents can't afford to take care of their children. They may decide to let someone adopt them to give their children a better life. The parent could be sick or too young, or the parents could have died."

"Why would a daddy and mama have a baby when they know they couldn't take care of it?"

"Maybe they thought they could. Sometimes things just happen and the only thing you can do is make it right.

"Why can't the grandfather and grandmother help?"

"I have seen a lot of grandfathers and grandmothers help raise their grandchildren without adoption. Also, I have seen uncles, aunts, family, and friends help too. But when there is no one to help, the only thing you can do is give the child up for adoption. Even though children may be happy with their new parents, they will always have an urge to see their real parents. They will not be satisfied until they see them. There is no love stronger than a parent's love. They will never stop loving their children. Love between parents and their children is strong and will never die."

"Yep, just like you and mama love me and I love y'all."

"That's right."

"I'm glad I'm not adopted. I don't want another daddy and mama."

"Adoption is a good thing. The parents that adopt children are very special. They want children to love, but they can't have children of their own or they want to take care of a child that needs love. Once they adopt them, they buy them new clothes, take them to church, feed them good, send them to school, help them do their homework, take them to the doctor, let them play with other children, and teach them right from wrong. I call adopted parents, and anyone who helps raise someone else's children, 'golden.' They have a special gift of love that came from God."

"What about the parents that gave them away?"

"They're golden too. It takes special parents to give their children to someone else to raise them better than they could. I pray for them because I know their hearts are hurting and wondering how their children are doing, what they look like, if they're happy, and if they made the right decision. I pray the adopted children don't hold any grudges against their parents for giving them up. I pray that no matter what the circumstances were for their adoption, they will always be loved by their parents. Also, I pray that all children understand that parents—or whoever is raising them—aren't perfect, and they make mistakes just like everybody else. Hopefully their adopted parents will teach them understanding and forgiveness."

"Do the adopted children have to do what their new parents tell them to do?

"Of course they do. The good book says, 'Honour thy father and thy mother: that thy days may be long upon the land which the Lord thy God giveth thee,' Exodus 20:12. The good book didn't say to honor just your real father and mother. A father and mother could be anyone who takes care of children and protects them. Children shouldn't talk about their father or mother in a bad way, whether they're living or dead. They shouldn't talk back to them, and they should listen to them because they know what's best for them."

"What if parents do something bad to the children?"

"All the parents I know are good to their children, but if there are parents who are bad to their children, God will take care of them. It doesn't matter if they're black, white, red, brown, or yellow—you can't do wrong and get by with it. The color of your skin won't save you. God is fair."

"What will God do?"

"Nobody knows God's plan, but I do know everything God does is for a good reason."

"Oooh."

"He's a mighty, good God."

"I do what you and Mama tell me to do, don't I, Daddy?"

"Yes, you do what we ask you to do. You're a good girl."

Daddy's approval of my behavior was all I needed to release the worry of God being disappointed in me. At a young age I knew that if I might live longer by honoring Daddy and Mama, I might not live long if I didn't.

"You know what, Daddy?"

"What, Edna?

"Now I know why Lynette was running like she was crazy when we were playing hopscotch. She didn't hop one time. She almost drove me crazy."

Daddy laughed so hard he cried and splattered his soda all over himself. It took him a few seconds to compose himself.

"Why do you think she was acting that way?"

"Because she's happy she has a daddy and mama. And she was glad to be outside playing. She probably hasn't played with anyone for a long time. I'm happy she has someone to love her."

"Yeah, you're probably right. I'm happy for her too. You did a good job figuring out Lynette."

Daddy gave me an appreciation for adoption and understanding of the importance of raising a child. Sharing his teaching verbally or through my actions has helped so many children and adults. When I meet people who have adopted children, I tell them they are "golden" and say how special they are. I support foster-care and adoption agencies, and donate to children with special needs to make sure no child is left out. Children are a blessing, and they should always be treated like a gift sent from heaven. Their little minds are innocent and they see the best in everyone. If we want our children to exhibit values like honesty, self-respect, and compassion for others, we need to show good qualities ourselves.

I taught my sons what I learned from Daddy and Mama. To maintain my sons' characters, I helped them using skillful and loving approaches. The skills I helped them with were built during normal interactions. Having meaningful conversations with them was just as important as laughing with them, playing with them, and spending quality time with them. Talking to my sons taught them to listen to others, consider other opinions, and care about others. When they saw me make an effort to have concern for others and an awareness of others' needs, they assumed that's just how things are done. Never once did I tell them what career to choose, and I reminded them on an ongoing basis of the following: "If you're happy, you can keep going, and if you keep going, you will be successful in the career you choose. If you base your career on how much money you can make, there is a greater chance of being unhappy, and money can't buy happiness."

What mattered to me most about my sons' development was that they live honestly, treat humanity with love and respect, and have faith and trust in God. Child-rearing can be difficult, but at the same time it can be rewarding. Sometimes what I taught them worked, and sometimes it didn't. When it doesn't work, experience can be the next best teacher. After years of career changes, stress, frustration, and unhappiness, they finally got what it takes to live a fulfilled life. They have always respected and shown so much love for me. They have also always shown love for others, and they go beyond expectations to keep peace among others, regardless of the situation. Love is what has kept my family intact for three generations. Daddy gave me a better understanding of God's purpose for parents and how valuable they are in a child's upbringing. It made me look at him and Mama in a different way. I'm thankful for what they did for me and I value their guidance. After the day I met Lynette, a day didn't go by that I didn't thank Daddy and Mama for everything they did for me. Even though they're in heaven, I still thank them everyday. They will always be my glory. They taught me that a parent and child's relationship represents the purpose for humanity. God created us because he wanted a family who would become like him and be in heaven with him. Parents are the key people in developing godly character in a child. Daddy and Mama developed my character by using the Bible. They loved teaching it. I take my role as a mother very seriously, and I used the Bible to help develop my sons too. My son takes his role as a father very seriously, and he uses the Bible to help him develop his daughters. And the teaching goes on. Soon there will be a fourth generation.

19

Black Patent Shoes

In September, 1964, at age fourteen, I was voted secretary for my eighth-grade homeroom class by the students in my classroom. Frank Shoffner was voted president, and Harold Smith was voted vice president. My classmates clapped when our names were announced and yelled, "Congratulations!" After Mrs. Lee announced the winners, I thanked the students for voting for me. I was honored to serve them and thankful they recognized my leadership and organizational and typing skills. At a young age, I typed seventy-five words per minute with no errors. The home keys were stuck in my head (a, s, d, f, g, h, j, k, l, and ;), and I could type anything blindfolded without worrying about not knowing where the keys were located. Typing was my ticket to success. I was thankful that I'd won because of my knowledge, performance, and dedication. The president, vice president, and I listened carefully while Mrs. Lee explained one of our responsibilities.

"The Christmas parade is scheduled for December 5 at 10:00 a.m. Even though we will have senior officers to represent the entire student body for Jordan Sellars, you will be riding in the parade to represent your homeroom class. We don't have to worry about a car to ride in the parade. My husband will let me drive his white 1960 Ford convertible, but we have to be careful and make sure it's clean when I take it back home. He loves his car. No eating or drinking in the car. We will make a sign for each side of the car with your names, the offices you hold, the grade you're in, your teacher's name, and 'Jordan Sellars High School' printed in bold letters. We're going to use our school colors. Edna, you have to wear a burgundy skirt, white top, and burgundy tam hat. The guys have to wear black pants, a white shirt, and a burgundy tam hat."

I was so excited, but not as excited as Daddy and Mama. They were proud of me being elected secretary of my classroom. They offered to help me in any way to make the parade a success, and they promised they would be at the parade to support me. Even though I was reluctant, I told them about the clothing I had to wear in the parade. Mama was a seamstress, but she didn't have any burgundy or white fabric left over from previous sewing projects. She had gone through every piece of fabric she had left, but was unsuccessful. Daddy smiled at me, looked at Mama, and left the room for a few minutes. Mama gave a sigh of relief because she knew what Daddy was about to do. He came back into the living room with a medium-sized leather pouch with drawstrings in his hand. He sat down beside Mama, pulled out some bills from the pouch, and laid them on the table.

"I was saving this money for a down payment to buy a house, but we're going to use some of it to take you shopping at Sellars Department Store."

"At Sellars Department Store?"

"Yes. We're going to buy you a skirt, blouse, and tam hat at Sellars."

"Oh my goodness!"

"Our daughter is going to have the best. Ain't nobody going to say you're wearing cheap clothes. You're going to have clothes from the best store in town. And that's not all. We're going to buy you a pair of black patent shoes and white socks to wear from H & K Bootery. It's the best shoe store in town. You're going to look like a princess."

I couldn't believe what I heard. Mama wore high-heel black patent shoes and carried a black patent pocketbook to church every Sunday. It made her clothes look so much better. She'd promised me that when Daddy had extra money, he would buy me the flat patent shoes I saw on display at H&K Bootery. My dream to own a pair of patent shoes had come true.

Was I dreaming? Was I in the right house? Spending money he saved up for a house on me? This was amazing!

"Oh my goodness! Thank you so much, Daddy. Thank you so much, Mama. When I get a job one day, I'm going to take y'all shopping."

I ran to my room, grabbed my pillow off my bed, and held it close as I danced and sang "Oh, What a Beautiful Mornin'" by Richard Rogers and Oscar Hammerstein II. It was a beautiful day because Daddy and Mama were proud of me. They were sure my caring personality had played a major role in my classmates voting for me.

Everybody in town knew that Sellars Department Store and H & K Bootery were upscale, expensive shopping stores. I had never shopped or imagined shopping in either place. On numerous occasions, I had walked downtown and window-shopped, pointing out clothing I would have one day. The dresses in the windows were almost as pretty as the ones Mama made for her customers. Mama could make the most beautiful dresses and suits without a pattern, and you couldn't tell they were homemade. Mama's dresses and suits were lined, carefully stitched, and fitted the customer's body perfectly. Every customer was satisfied, and they kept coming back even though they could afford to purchase clothing in upscale clothing stores. Mama was in demand.

I was amazed when I walked inside Sellars with Daddy and Mama. It was everything I had imagined. The environment in the store was carefully crafted. Every detail in the store grabbed my attention, including the antique, bronze manual elevator. The elevator was controlled by an African American operator who used his hand for speed and direction. The mannequins, located at the front of each section, had colorful outfits on their slim figures, and the graphically designed background put everything in place. Beautiful jewelry was displayed in clear glass showcases throughout the store, and a very pleasant salesclerk greeted every customer that came into the store with a smile. Mama and I had so much to choose from, including hair accessories, head pieces, and underwear. Daddy found a chair to sit in near the bathroom while Mama helped me try on different outfits.

When we walked into H & K Bootery, I saw the shoes I wanted instantly. They were the shoes I had seen in magazines and catalogues. I was overjoyed that the owner of the store gave me a pair of white, pink, and blue socks to go with my pretty black patent shoes. I had tears of joy when Mama selected a black patent purse for me to take to the parade. In each store, after I decided what I wanted to wear, Mama showed it to Daddy for his approval. Daddy had a piece of paper and pencil on his knee to add up all the items. The clothing, shoes, and purse we selected must have been within his budget because he approved everything with pride, including Mama's nylon, seam-free stockings. I had so much fun shopping at Sellars and H & K Bootery, and I will never forget the superior service we received from the owners and salesclerks. They treated us like royalty. Daddy made sure I had the best for the parade in spite of a limited budget.

"Are you happy?"

"I'm very happy, Daddy."

"Good."

Mama gave Daddy a loving smile.

On the day of the parade, Mama helped me get dressed and hot-combed my hair straight, then styled it with a beautiful burgundy bow on each side of my head, leaving room in the middle of my hair for the tam. Daddy warmed my white socks, carefully put my warm socks and shoes on my feet, and had me turn around slowly to make sure the socks were pulled up evenly.

"You could be on a magazine cover. You look like a little princess."

"Thank you, Daddy."

He didn't have time to tell a story because we had to be downtown early. I was on cloud nine and ready for the world to see me. It was the biggest event that had ever happened to me as a young teenager. My expensive wool top, wool skirt, purse, and shoes made a difference in how I looked, and my self-esteem was higher than ever. There was nothing I felt I couldn't do.

Mrs. Lee's eyes lit up when she saw me get out of Daddy's car.

"You look marvelous! I almost didn't recognize you."

"Thank you."

She reached into her pocketbook and pulled out a pair of white knit gloves for me and black knit gloves for Frank and Harold.

"I forgot to tell y'all to wear gloves, so I bought them for you. It's chilly out here and I don't want you getting a cold."

"Thank you, Mrs. Lee. Can we keep the gloves when the parade is over?"

"Of course you can, Edna."

Frank and Harold were just as excited as I was to have new gloves.

"Thank you, Mrs. Lee."

"You're welcome, Frank."

"Thank you, Mrs. Lee."

"You're welcome, Harold."

Frank and Harold escorted me to the parade car and opened the door for me. They treated me like a sister by being overprotective, considerate, respectful, and courageous. They even followed me to the bathroom and stood by the door until I came out to make sure I was safe. We were a team. The cars, trucks, and floats were lined up based on number assignments, and the clowns, cartoon characters, and bands walked in between the vehicles and at the rear of the parade. There was participation from retail stores, organizations, business owners, the fire department, trained horses, classic cars, and dance groups dressed in different holiday costumes or holiday T-shirts with logos. Santa Claus and his helpers were throwing hard candy to the spectators, and Mrs. Santa Claus was walking behind Santa giving hugs to the children. Daddy, Mama, my family members, and other spectators waved at us as our car drove slowly through town. Mama kept throwing me kisses and Daddy kept waving until I was out of sight. It was obvious they were enjoying every minute of the parade. People were running up to the cars taking pictures, including the local newspaper photographer. Our classmates were screaming out our names and running down the side of the street following us until exhaustion took over. When we returned to our designated drop-off area, Frank and Harold opened the door for me and didn't leave until Daddy and Mama picked me up. It was wonderful to see so many people at the parade to support us, and it was exciting to take part in making the parade a success. My suggestions, ideas, and hard work were appreciated. Having the experience working on the farm and representing my class in the parade confirmed that my purpose was leading, influencing team performance, and setting goals to get amazing results. Also, I knew that in order to be successful, I had to lead with compassion, communication, coaching, and counseling. That special time in my life will always be cherished and held close to my heart. I'm thankful I have a lasting, positive memory of a sweet man I was proud to call Daddy. It was the last time I rode in a parade and the last time Daddy took me shopping.

20

Something Is Wrong

It was in the middle of January 1965 when I noticed that Daddy was biting his nails a lot. He slept longer than before and was taking pills his doctor had prescribed for him. He was deep in thought, quieter than usual, and seemed troubled. At the time, I didn't think much of it and didn't know what was lying ahead. Several times I saw him go outside in the cold weather and sit on the porch, looking up at the sky or taking a walk back and forth across the yard. At night he would go out onto the front porch, watch the stars in the sky, and hum a song I wasn't familiar with. Mama would go out onto the porch with him for a short while to talk, and then they both would come back into the house, shivering from the cold weather. Neither one of them offered any explanations for his sudden behavioral and psychological changes. His kindness and love for his family stayed intact, and he never missed a day of work so he could provide for us. Sometimes after he came home from work, I found him reading the Bible at the kitchen table or playing his harmonica in their bedroom. For the first time, I looked at him closely. So many things were running through my head that my body couldn't keep up with my thought processes. For some reason, I felt that whatever was going on with him, I couldn't do anything about it.

"Is it his job?"

"Did somebody hurt his feeling?"

"Is he worried about us?"

I was feeling down and exhausted because I didn't know what was wrong and I didn't know how to make Daddy feel better. Mama was in her sewing room making a beautiful quilt for a baby's crib when I entered the room quietly. She didn't take her eyes off the quilt as I began asking questions.

"Mama, is Daddy okay?"

"Yes, why?"

"Well, he's acting different."

"How is he acting different?"

"He's sleeping a lot and he doesn't talk much."

"He's been working really hard these past few days."

"Ohhhh."

"He's not talking much because he's tired and he isn't feeling well."

"Is that why he's taking those pills?"

Mama took her eyes off the quilt and raised her eyes at me. Even when she tried to get tough, her gentleness wouldn't allow her to raise her voice. Her spiritual, angelic personality was always beautiful, pure, and virtuous even when she tried to scold me.

"I hope you haven't been snooping around in our bedroom? You know that's not nice."

"No, Mama! I saw him swallow the pills with a glass of water in the kitchen."

"Okay. Glad to know you're a good girl."

Somehow, Mama got off the subject of Daddy and starting talking about getting me to make a quilt.

"Edna, do you still want to make a quilt for your bed?"

"Yes ma'am."

"Good! I want you to look at the large scraps of different material I have left and pick different colors you want for the front of your quilt. After you pick your colors, you are going to cut out squares to make the front of your quilt."

"Really?"

"Yes. I'm going to show you how to measure the squares so they will all be the same size. I have everything you need right here. In the closet, I have different-color fabric for the back of the quilt that will match. We don't have to buy anything."

There were so many items in the sewing box, on the sewing machine, and on the floor, and lots of fabric in several long, huge plastic storage bins up against the walls.

"What is all that other stuff?"

"All that other stuff is thread, sharp scissors, rulers, a cutting board, pins, seam rippers, needles, tracers, thimbles, and tracing papers."

"Wow!"

"When I finish this quilt, we will start on yours. Now, are you sure you want to make yourself a quilt?"

"Yes ma'am. I'm sure."

"Okay. You have to have a lot of patience."

"I do."

When Mama looked directly at me and nodded her head, I knew she was convinced that I was ready to take on making a quilt. I was tired of cutting and sewing simplicity patterns. Talking to Mama about the steps in making my quilt took my mind off Daddy, at least for a little while.

After unsuccessfully trying to get information from Mama and getting frustrated from trying to figure out what was wrong on my own, I decided to ask Daddy. When I found him outside stacking wood in the woodshed, I felt he needed me to help him. He wasn't moving as usual, and he rested after each trip to the woodshed. For a few minutes, I watched him closely. He was the most perfect man I had seen in my life, and I had an inherent hunger for his fatherly love. He was strong and courageous, and no one would bully or harm me because he would stomp them into the ground if they hurt me. At least, that's what I wanted him to do and I didn't have any problem making the bullies believe he would do it. They wouldn't come ten feet close to me if they were up to no good. Daddy protected me and everyone else in his presence from forces that threatened us. He was my all-knowing and all-powerful daddy. For some unknown reason, I feared the worst. I felt anxious all the time, and I needed reassurance to feel soothed. First Peter 5:6–7 didn't calm me the least bit: "Humble yourselves therefore under the mighty hand of God, that he may exalt you in due time: Casting all your care upon him; for he careth for you."

"Daddy, do you need any help?"

"No, I'm almost finished."

"I can bring the wood to the shed while you're resting."

"I have rested enough. I don't have but one more pile to bring in. Thanks anyway."

"But I want to help."

"It's cold out here. I didn't warm your socks before you came out. You need to get back in the house before you get a cold. I will be finished in a few minutes."

"Are you coming in the house when you finish?"

"I'll be in shortly."

When Daddy came into the house, I was waiting at the back door to talk to him.

"Daddy, do your legs hurt?"

"No. What makes you think my legs hurt?"

"You walk slow and you have to rest a lot."

"Well, I rest because I'm tired, and when you're tired you can't walk as fast as you used to."

"Ohhh. Is that why you take pills—so you won't be tired anymore?"

Daddy's puzzled frown made me answer his question before he asked it, because I didn't want him thinking I was deliberately being sneaky.

"I didn't go snooping in your bedroom. I saw you take some pills in the kitchen."

Just like Mama, he avoided answering the question and began talking about me worrying too much.

"Don't worry about me. How many times have I told you that worrying gets you nowhere? All it does is make you sick. It makes you not think right, it makes things worse than they are, and it can't change anything. If it's God's will, he will change things, and if it's not his will, he won't change them. So why worry your pretty little head? You need to enjoy being a teenager and all the goodness God has for you. You can't enjoy it worrying. Do you remember the verse I read to you in the good book about the birds?"

"No sir."

"It says, 'Behold the fowls of the air: for they sow not, neither do they reap, nor gather into barns; yet your heavenly Father feedeth them. Are ye not much better than they?' Matthew 6:26. Do you know why they don't store food away in the barn?"

"No sir."

"They don't worry about having enough food because they know God is going to take care of them and make sure they have food to eat. They spend their time enjoying flying thousands of miles to view different countries, cities, oceans, rivers, trees, flowers, people, and animals. When winter comes, they don't need warm socks because they fly to warmer places. They're happy, and I want you to be happy too."

Daddy was so good at finding the right words to explain any subject or concern, and he explained precisely and eloquently. My anxiety ceased and my understanding of the Bible advanced. Daddy's daily routine went back to normal, or at least it seemed that way. I never saw him take another pill. He was walking normally again, not sleeping as much, and "talking up a storm." Sometimes when I look back at his suddenly improved health, I wonder if his health really improved or if he was protecting me by pretending he was back to normal again. Only God knew the answer, a verse Daddy quoted many times: "For if our heart condemn us, God is greater than our heart, and knoweth all things" (1 John 3:20). My brain was exhausted from trying to figure out if Daddy was really alright, so I let go of my suspicion.

21

Goodbye, Sweet Daddy

On February 22, 1965, my protected, secure, and peaceful world came tumbling down. It was an awakening to how unpredictable life can be and how nothing, no matter how precious, will last forever.

Television was a reward on the weekends when I had completed household chores for the week, studied, passed weekly tests, and obeyed Daddy and Mama on an ongoing basis. Daddy usually selected the television programs to use as a tool to motivate learning and increase awareness. The outcome of his selections always impacted me in a positive way. Because I had put extra effort into household chores that week, he reluctantly approved my request to watch *Cinderella*. All my classmates were talking about watching *Cinderella* and how good the love story was going to be. I didn't want to miss it. Watching a story about a kindhearted girl who suffered many hardships and married the prince of the kingdom gave me the hope of one day marrying a hero. After all, I was crushing on an intelligent and handsome "hunk" guy in school. He just didn't know it, and neither did Daddy and Mama. It was a secret I kept all throughout school.

I turned on the television at the scheduled time and relaxed on the recliner with a glass of milk and a piece of apple pie. I was enjoying watching *Cinderella* while Mama was relaxing on the couch. She was burned out from cooking a big dinner. She was almost asleep when we heard a knock on the front door. It was Miss Mary, our next door neighbor, who the community looked up to and trusted. Frantically, she asked me to step outside.

"Your daddy was found dead on the path near your house. They think he had a heart attack while he was walking home."

I was weak, speechless, and confused, and didn't know what to do. I looked at Miss Mary, almost falling down. I couldn't believe she'd said it so matter-of-factly. Miss Mary realized I wasn't as strong and courageous as I had seemed. She held me up and guided me back to the living room. I looked over at the kitchen table, which was arranged eloquently. My girlish mind felt that it was impossible for Daddy to be dead because Mama had his dinner waiting for him. She had beautiful cross-stitch towels over the biscuits, roast beef, stewed corn, turnip greens, and apple pie to keep his meal warm. Daddy loved coming home to a delicious meal with warm, homemade biscuits. He never missed eating at home, and he wouldn't leave us without saying goodbye.

"This can't be true. I have to go outside and check for myself. Daddy said to never listen to one side of a story."

Before I reached the front door, the policeman knocked at the door. When I opened it, I saw the police car parked in front of the house. The blue lights were flashing and the neighbors were gathering in our yard, crying and comforting each other. I didn't want to hear what he was going to say.

The policeman told Mama that Daddy was dead and they had sent someone to get his body. I remember Mama crying hysterically and Miss Mary comforting her. When I heard them ask Mama what funeral home she wanted Daddy transported to, I gasped.

"Take him to Sharpe Funeral Home."

I ran to my room and fell on the floor before making it to my bed. I couldn't go any further. I was angry. I was fourteen years old and didn't understand why he had to die.

In the middle of the night, I made my way to the bed and laid on top of the covers. I tossed and turned all night long. The next day I got up and started getting ready for school.

"Daddy would want me to go to school and pass my test. He will be home when I get back. I know he will."

"Where are you going, Edna?"

"I'm going to school?

"You can't go to school."

"Why can't I?"

"Because Herbert died last night. You have to stay home to pay respects to your daddy."

"Daddy is left alone in that funeral home! Mama, you need to go and get him and bring him back home. He's all alone."

"He's gone to heaven with God. I can't bring him back home."

I threw a pillow from the sofa and began screaming. Mama let me scream until I couldn't scream anymore. She held me tightly in her arms, kissing me repeatedly on my forehead. When I felt her tears drip down my neck, I hugged her and kissed her on her cheek. We were in mourning together over the death of a precious man who loved us deeply.

The *Burlington Daily Times* news headline read:

MAN FOUND DEAD LAST NIGHT

Berkeley Herbert Brown, 47 years old Negro of Burlington was found dead on a path near his home last night at about 8:45 pm. Alamance County Coroner ruled that death was due to natural causes. The Burlington Fire Department set up lights in the area at about 9:00 pm to make an investigation after the body was recovered. Mr. Brown was a native of Caswell County and an employee of Alamance County Schools. He was a member of Blackwell Baptist Church. Survivors are his wife, Willie Elizabeth Long Brown . . .[3]

"They have the wrong person. This person isn't Daddy. How could it be? The man that's dead is forty-seven. Daddy just had a birthday this past July. He said he was forty-six years old. We had cake and ice cream and sang happy birthday to him. This has to be a mistake. Daddy will be coming home soon."

Reality gradually kicked in when Daddy didn't come home that night and when I saw him in his coffin at the viewing. There were lots of colorful flowers on the floor on each side of his coffin and in front of it. I knew from his appearance that he hadn't dressed himself. He had on his Sunday suit, a starched white shirt, and a black tie. His eyes were closed and his lips weren't moving. He was lying on his back in the gray metal coffin, lifeless. He never wore a starched shirt, and he slept on his right side. He never slept any other way. I wanted to stay with him, but a church member took me by the hand and sat me down beside Mama. I watched familiar and unfamiliar faces walk up to the coffin to stare at Daddy. Some of them softly cried and some of them were silent. Each of them greeted us with a hug or handshake and a sympathy card, and offered support when needed. I was exhausted and felt relieved when the viewing was over. I wanted to go home and talk with God. God was my only hope. That night I began bargaining with God to return Daddy back to me.

"Dear God, please bring Daddy back. I promise to be good and do all my homework. I will clean up, wash the dishes, wash our clothes, and help the neighbors. I will do whatever you want me to do. Please God, I need Daddy and I know he wants to be home with us. He doesn't need to be at the funeral home with those people. They don't love him like I do. Please God, please! I know you can do it. I know you can."

I had faith that he would be back home when I woke up the next morning because Daddy had read me the Bible story about Jesus raising the dead: "Jesus said unto her, thy brother shall rise again. Martha saith unto him, I know that he shall rise again in the resurrection at the last day. Jesus said unto her, I am the resurrection and life: he that believeth in me, though he was dead, yet shall he live: And whosoever liveth and believeth in me shall never die. Believest thou this?" (John 11:23–26). During that time, I didn't understand that Daddy's body would be buried in his grave, but his spiritual body would be raised up (1 Cor 15:37, 42–44).

The next morning, I ran into Mama's and Daddy's bedroom and he wasn't there. Mama was sleeping, holding her opened Bible in her hands. It was evident she had been crying all night. Dry tears were on her face and on the upper area of the sheet next to her chin. I was furious and depressed because Daddy wasn't with Mama. I ran back to my bedroom, slammed the door, and fell on my bed, almost hitting the bed pole.

"Why did you have to take Daddy, God? He didn't do anything bad to people. He loved you and he read the Bible all the time. He went to church and prayed every night. He worked hard and took care of us. He warmed my socks to make sure my feet were warm. He said nice things about every-body, even when they were mean to him. He put all his trust in you and he said you would never let him down. God, I don't understand why he had to die. Why? Why? Why?"

I was drained from crying and began feeling a dull, achy sensation at the front of my head. I felt pressure in my abdomen and I was nauseated. After I kept gagging, I ran to the bathroom and vomited into the toilet. I had made myself sick, and I was afraid to tell Mama. She didn't need to worry about anything else, and she needed me. I thought about what Daddy had done when he accidentally shut the truck door on his hand. Just like him, I slowly breathed in and out until I was relaxed. The difference was that his pain went away and my pain would last a lifetime. Falling to sleep was difficult the first night after his death, and I woke up crying often during the night. The next morning, I felt like I hadn't slept at all. I was sleepy and agitated. People came in and out of the house all day with food, drinks, monetary gifts, and flowers. Mama was weak, but her weakness never made her mistreat anyone. She greeted and hugged friends, family members, and strangers as soon as they walked into the house. We had never had so many people in our house at one time. The house was so crowded that there was very minimal empty space between people. I wanted everyone to go home and stop saying the same words over and over again.

"What happened to him?"

"I'm so sorry for your loss."

"He's in a better place."

"He's not suffering anymore."

"I know exactly what you're going through."

"You look tired."

"You need to eat for your strength."

At that young age, I didn't know their actions were cultural behaviors to express how much they thought of us. They came because they loved Daddy too, and they wanted to make sure we weren't alone during the mourning process. They brought food so Mama wouldn't have to cook, and they washed dishes, cleaned the kitchen table, emptied the trash cans, swept the floors, and supervised the visitors. I don't know how we would have made it without family and friends. They were a blessing to us.

For a while, I became stoic. Next, I pretended like nothing had happened. I convinced myself it was just a dream. Being in denial was working for me—I created an imaginary world. I went upstairs to the attic and pretended I was having tea with Daddy.

"Daddy, do you prefer coffee or tea?"

"I should've known you were going to say coffee. You always drink coffee."

"I'm having tea and cookies. Do you want a cookie?"

"Okay, you can have a cookie."

I pretended I was drinking, eating cookies, and talking to Daddy. I imagined he was at the table with me enjoying his coffee and butter cookie. I didn't realize I had fallen asleep with my head on the table until Mama yelled for me to come downstairs. I hoped I was dreaming and that Daddy would be downstairs waiting for me to help in the kitchen. Hope soon faded into despair.

"Daddy isn't here. He's gone, and he won't be back."

I was permanently out of denial and had come to terms with Daddy's death at an early age of fourteen. There were no words to describe what I was feeling, and I didn't know what was going to happen to me. I was afraid of the world he had protected me from, and I didn't trust anyone but Mama.

"I hope Mama can make it without Daddy. She isn't herself and she cries all the time. Oh my goodness! What if something happens to her? What if she gets sick and can't take care of me? What if she dies too? God, please don't let her die too. I don't want to be adopted and live with someone else. I would run away. "

The next morning the house was crowded with family and friends, including Milton and Hilda. They were cooking breakfast, greeting people at the door, and helping Mama and me get ready for the funeral. I didn't complain about anything, and the dress attire that was selected for me to wear didn't matter. Nothing mattered to me anymore. Mama called me into the living room, where a big, tall African American man was standing in the middle of the floor. He was friendly, sympathetic, and professional. He passed out the obituary to all of us, giving instructions at the same time. He began giving instructions for us to get in line to ride in the funeral hearse.

"Get in line when I call your name if you are the family of Berkeley Herbert Brown. First, his spouse. Next in line are the children, parents, sisters, brothers, uncles, aunts, nephews, nieces. Everybody else will have to drive your own cars. Turn on your headlights and follow the hearse."

"What a foolish man," I thought. I didn't feel comfortable with him in the house because he didn't know what relatives Daddy had. "Daddy doesn't have any brothers, and Grandma and Grandpa are dead."

As our names were called, we walked quietly to the hearse and sat in our designated seat. Another African American man was standing by the hearse, making sure we were following instructions. He helped me step up into the hearse and shut all the hearse doors. He stood straight and tall like a statue, and he didn't move until everyone was in the hearse. As the driver slowly drove to the funeral home chapel, vehicles pulled off the side of the road to show their respect. There was no conversation between us while riding to the funeral. All the tissues the driver had given us were used before we arrived at the funeral home. We cried all the way. When we entered the funeral home chapel, the congregation stood up to honor us. We were led to the front row by a church usher. The flower girls and pallbearers sat on the right side of the church, and the pastor and speaker sat behind the podium facing the congregation. Familiar and unfamiliar faces were crying, and some of them were consoling others. Nurses and ushers were standing at the front, in the middle, and at the back of the chapel passing out tissues and paper fans when they were needed. Everybody I remembered during the service had on black dresses or suits except for the ushers. They had on white dresses and wore white gloves. When the choir sang "Amazing Grace," Mama cried so hard the nurse had to help her up to view Daddy's body. She was tired and troubled by Daddy's death, and I was no help to her. I was exhausted from lack of sleep, and I could barely walk because of weakness in my legs. Reverend Thomas preached and a church member read some of the cards people had sent to the church to be read to the family. The cards were words of sympathy and inspiration. After the funeral had concluded, the funeral director closed the coffin. He led the pallbearers carrying the coffin out to the hearse. Our driver followed the hearse to the grave site, which was located in Reidsville, North Carolina. Riding through thirty miles of beautiful nature would have been a scenic ride if Daddy had been driving us. The appearance of the sky, trees, and bushes looked dreary, almost like they were in mourning too. It was the most horrible ride ever because I knew I would never see Daddy again. I wanted the driver to turn around and take Daddy back home, but he kept driving because it was his job. It seemed like he was oblivious to our hurt and pain. How could he understand the impact of our loss? He didn't know how dedicated and committed Daddy had been to us. Daddy didn't belong in a dark grave, even though he wasn't afraid of the dark like me. He was brave and nothing frightened him. I will never forget the song that was playing on the radio on our way to Daddy's grave: "You've Lost That Lovin' Feeling'" by the Righteous Brothers. The Righteous Brothers' voices ricocheted through my body and the sound of their music gave me mixed emotions. I couldn't stop crying. When we arrived at the grave site, we were led to the folding chairs under the funeral-home tent to be seated. Reverend Thomas prayed and placed a rose on top of Daddy's coffin.

"Ashes to ashes, dust to dust."

Those were the last words I heard at Daddy's grave site. Daddy was laid to rest, and he wouldn't be coming back home with us.

"Goodbye, sweet Daddy. I love you."

After the burial, the congregation provided a meal for us even though we didn't have appetites. There were so many people in the dining room eating, laughing, and talking like nothing had happened. Mama was quiet and distraught, and she barely touched her food.

"How dare they enjoy themselves knowing Daddy was in the ground and can't talk or eat! Daddy, I wish you were here to take me home."

It was hard for me to understand their behavior, and I was afraid I was going to yell at someone if we didn't leave soon.

"Daddy would be disappointed in me and Mama doesn't need anything else to worry about. Jesus, please help me keep my mouth shut."

I didn't realize they didn't know what to say or how to respond to our loss. We finally left the church and returned home to emptiness, helplessness, fear, and loneliness.

After many sleepless nights, prayers, and days with no appetite, I opened Daddy's Bible and searched for verses to comfort and heal me. Daddy said God is the father of mercies and doesn't want his children to suffer. "Blessed are they that mourn: for they shall be comforted (Matt 5:4); "Come unto me, all ye that labour and are heavy laden, and I will give you rest. Take my yoke upon you, and learn of me; for I am meek and lowly in heart: and ye shall find rest unto your souls. For my yoke is easy, and burden is light" (Matt 11:28–30); "And all things, whatsoever ye shall ask in prayer, believing, ye shall receive" (Matt 21:22).

Somehow, the verses eased my pain. Several nights after the funeral, a warm sensation around my waist suddenly woke me up from a restless sleep. It gradually penetrated my body. It was a powerful feeling I had never experienced before. Reluctantly, I rose from my bed and stiffened when I saw an image of Daddy standing at the foot of my bed. He was centered in a bright light and his bright copper skin was beautiful and glowed throughout my bedroom in the darkness. The candle on the nightstand had blown out. Daddy had on bib overalls with a navy-blue, long-sleeve shirt and a straw hat tipped on the right side of his head. He smiled at me and said, "I'm alright." Before I could say anything, he was gone. The minute he disappeared, the candle lit up. I wasn't afraid but happy he had appeared before me to free me from worry. I felt like a burden had been lifted off my shoulders, and I slept peacefully that night without tossing and turning. I knew Daddy was okay. The next morning I started questioning myself about my magical experience.

"Was I dreaming? Did I really see Daddy?"

When I got up from bed, I noticed a pair of white socks on the floor. Mama had given me blue socks to wear and I remembered putting them in the dirty-laundry basket before going to bed.

"I would never put clean socks on the floor. Maybe Mama accidentally dropped them."

When I picked the socks up from the floor, I was startled because the socks were warm, but with a different type of warmth. The socks felt just like the powerful warmth I'd felt around my waist, and holding them gave me a calm feeling.

"Oh my God, Daddy was here with me last night. Daddy, I miss you."

I buried my face in the socks and wept until the warmth had left. There was no doubt in my mind that I had seen a vision of Daddy and that he had left the warm socks on the floor. Even though he was gone from my sight, I knew he would be with me always. He validated that he was the one who had watched over me that night by leaving the warm socks. I had no stove in my bedroom, and there was no fire in the kitchen stove that morning. He answered my questions like he always did, but this time in a different way to release my emotional stress over his death. That was the one and only vision I had of Daddy after his death, but I sense his presence around me, especially when I'm feeling blue. No more restless sleep, no more anger, and no more feeling sorry for myself.

"Thank you, Daddy, for always taking care of me."

I still cry when I hear the Righteous Brothers' song because it is so true that I lost a loving feeling. Their lyrics don't just remind me of Daddy's death or the warm-socks confirmation—the song is a reminder that Daddy's death wasn't the end but instead the beginning of being in heaven with God, his heavenly father. "Then shall the dust return to the earth as it was: and the spirit shall return unto God who gave it" (Eccl 12:7).

Daddy is still everything to me, and my love for him has never died. He lives forever in my heart and he is in everything I do. Everything Daddy did was done in love for his family and humanity. I'm thankful to God for giving me a wonderful, loving, and generous Daddy who taught me what was necessary in order to have a peaceful and fulfilled life. He was only here with me for a short period of time, but his life lessons are instilled in me for a lifetime. He saw the best in me and I see the best in my children. I constantly remind them that they are special and how proud I am of them. I teach them to appreciate themselves, never want to be like anyone else, enjoy the simple things of life, find their own happiness, and never let go of their faith in God. All the people I wanted to be like and everyone else in this beautiful world aren't better than me. How could they be better when God created us all? None of us is perfect, and most of us are far from it. My loving and caring parents were a gift God gave me. Because Daddy died at an early age, I blamed him for leaving us. If he had had a choice, I thought, he would have stayed. Now I know that even though I had him for a short while, he taught me a wealth of knowledge about life, honesty, and Christianity. Material things will come and go, but what he instilled in me will last forever. My father wasn't rich or powerful. He wasn't a famous artist, a doctor, or a lawyer. He was a man of God who served his purpose on earth by spreading the word of God to his family and to all who would listen. He didn't have a college degree, but he earned a humanity degree from God for a job well done. It's the only degree you can take with you when you leave this world. I know he's in heaven smiling down right now. Because the Bible says so, I know God has wiped away all his tears, and he doesn't have to cry anymore. He has no more sorrow and no more pain, and he will die no more. He's happy all the time (Rev 21:4).

"Daddy, I'm forever grateful. Thank you for your never-ending love. I miss you warming my socks. You always made me feel like somebody. You're the best!"

Deep down I experienced trouble with my self-esteem, and I had difficulty bonding in relationships in my early years because I didn't want to love someone and lose them in death. Through prayer, I overcame my psychological distress. Today, I still struggle with coping with death, especially if the person is family. Even though death is ugly, it's a process of life. I don't try to make it palatable with pious platitudes. Instead, I ponder, trying to understand the purpose of dying. Sometimes I find myself asking God why he didn't stop my loved ones from dying when he had the power to do so. Several of my Christian friends have told me I shouldn't question God because "it's a sin." How could asking God an honest question be a sin? To me, asking God when you're troubled is believing in him. It's the right thing to do because God doesn't tell lies. I may not get an answer, but I know I didn't get it for a good reason.

I didn't have Daddy at my graduation to cheer me on, like so many others did. I wish he could have been there when I had my first heartbreak, when I got married, and when I gave birth to my two sons. Mama took lead of the household after Daddy died and she was by my side through all my ups and downs. Effortlessly, Mama did a magnificent job raising me with love, teaching me, listening and understanding me, showing me compassion, and praying for me. She ensured that I had a loving, Christian, safe, and peaceful home. She lived long enough for people to see how wonderful she was and how much she loved and had faith in God. She had the purest soul and was known for helping and caring for others. I never saw her angry or hold a grudge, and she never grumbled about her problems. Her gentle, warm heart is mentioned to this day. Many people didn't have the opportunity to know Daddy because of his short, private life. He was a good husband and father. He was patient, worthy of respect, dignified, proud, self-controlled, and an undervalued hard worker. In addition, he was honest, not a lover of money, and a mentor, and he manifested the fruits of the spirit. He wanted me to be a nurse to take care of people. I didn't become a nurse, but I did work in the health-care system for Hutzel Hospital in Detroit, Michigan (business manager), UNC Health Care in Chapel Hill, North Carolina (clinic manager), and Piedmont Health SeniorCare in Burlington, North Carolina (operations manager, site manager, and medical records manager) for a total of forty years. I took care of thousands of patients in an indirect way, and I know Daddy is proud of me.

I know Daddy and Mama are in heaven enjoying its splendor, glory, beauty, and majesty. Daddy is probably playing beautiful gospel music on his harmonica and helping the little children in heaven with Mama at his side. I feel strongly that when Daddy arrived in heaven, God said, "In spite of your struggles, you were a good husband and father. You didn't listen to the faith-killers. Well done, good and faithful servant."

I'm also thankful that God loves me unconditionally. Even though it took me many years, I finally got the message. God was patient with me and waited patiently for me to understand his purpose for me. He protects, provides, guides, and has a plan for me. He gives me power to stand, preservation, salvation, provision, and glorification. I'm so blessed by and appreciative of his love.

A day doesn't go by that I don't think about the young woman I met in the waiting room. I'm sure that if it's in God's plan, I will see her again. "For I know the thoughts that I think toward you, saith the Lord, thoughts of peace, and not evil, to give you an expected end" (Jer 29:11). I pray she will find peace in her heart to forgive her father for the emotional and physical abuse he caused her to endure. I pray for him to find peace within and embrace her with love. I pray for her to heal and use her experience to help someone else. I pray that she learn about God and his son, Jesus Christ, and accept him as her Savior. I also pray that she will embrace the Scriptures and that her life will be filled with love, joy, and happiness. Praying is powerful. She was off to a good start when she accepted the Bible. The Bible is necessary in our lives to teach us the Christian way to live so that we can have everlasting life. I'm looking forward to seeing Daddy, Mama, family members, and friends in heaven one day. It will be a day of rejoicing. Daddy and Mama showed me by their actions and teachings that love is the greatest gift of all. God is love, and with love, everything is possible! It took both of them to instill love in me and I'm so happy they did! Daddy did fulfill his role as husband and father. My treasures aren't what Daddy gave me—they're what he taught me. I'm blessed God gave me parents who brought me up with spiritual discipline and instructions of God.

22

It's What He Taught Me

The fresh air and beautiful trees surrounding me outside the clinic increased my mood of happiness and appreciation of my parents' powerful love. My spirit was uplifted. For the first time in a while, the lessons Daddy had taught me from the Bible gave me the desire to seek spiritual growth and increase my knowledge and understanding of God's word. My negative thoughts and worries faded away, and I had no more desires for material things or the "elite society." Being outdoors enhanced my ability to think about ways to serve humanity.

"Daddy would be proud of me if I taught God's word to others. Maybe I can volunteer in senior homes or do personal shopping for them."

Nothing I thought of pleased or satisfied me. There was something my subconscious was trying to tell me I needed to do. Two beautiful red cardinals flew to a tree nearby and sat on a broken limb dangling from the tree. The uniqueness of their chirping made me realize there was something special about them. When I stood up, they didn't fly away. Instead, they gracefully sat up straight from their hunched-over posture, with their tails pointed straight down. Their chirping changed to whistling sounds. An overwhelming sensation spread throughout my body. The sensation was so powerful I began crying. Suddenly, I felt a spiritual presence near me with an important message. I didn't ignore the message because I knew God sent this message to me.

I closed my eyes and began praying: "God, I'm sorry I ignored your messages in the past. It will never happen again. I'm going to take care of it right now."

When I looked up at the tree to see and hear the cardinals' whistle again, they were gone. Immediately, I began dialing my friend Rita to ask for a favor.

I had just ended my conversation with Rita when someone touched me on my back. I jumped from fright. Joann put her arms around me to calm me down. She knew it didn't take much to frighten me.

"Edna, I'm so sorry. I didn't mean to scare you. Are you alright?"

"Yes, I'm fine. I was occupied. I didn't see you walk up behind me."

"I'm so excited! My physical went well. My blood work was perfect, blood pressure 120/70, temperature 97.8, pulse 80, and oxygen saturation 100!"

"Wow, Joann! I'm proud of you. What about your weight?"

"I'm not going to talk about it because I don't want to hear you preach."

"Joann, I promise not to preach. I'm taking you out to lunch. You can order whatever you want to eat."

"What?"

"That's right."

"What has happened to you? Are you the Edna I know? The Edna I know would never tell me to get whatever I want. As a matter of fact, the Edna I know doesn't let me eat in peace. She has something to say about everything I put in my mouth."

"I'm not going to say anything else while you're eating. Joann, I have another plan to help us lose weight. We're going to lose weight slowly by eating right and exercising. Once every two weeks you need to treat yourself. You deserve it especially after getting a good report today."

"I want to go to Longhorn Steakhouse. I love eating there. Can I order a six-ounce Renegade Sirloin and Redrock Grilled Shrimp with broccoli? I haven't been there since I've been laid off from work."

"Yes, you can order your steak and shrimp, or anything you want."

"Wow! Thank you so much, Edna."

"Joann, I have some good news for you."

"What?"

"You will be working soon. I found a job for you."

"Oh my God! Edna, are you serious?"

"My friend Rita needs a supervisor/cook to manage the kitchen in her restaurant. Joann, you have the experience and you're a good cook. It's full-time with good pay. They offer health insurance, vacation and sick time, and holiday pay. I told her you would call her to confirm your 9:00 a.m. appointment tomorrow to make it official. I'm going to take you to your appointment. I will give you her telephone number when we get to Longhorn."

"I don't know what to say. Wait a minute!"

"What is it, Joann?"

"I don't have a car."

"Yes you do, Joann."

"No I don't, Edna!"

"Joann, you will be driving the car in my garage that is collecting dust. It's thirteen years old, but it runs well. I'm giving you the car and I will loan you money for the insurance, taxes, and tags. You can pay me back the loan a little at a time. If you have to miss a payment, I'll know you missed it for a good reason. I will understand."

"Edna, are you serious?"

"Yes, Joann. That's what friends are for."

"Edna, catch me! I'm about to pass out."

"You can't pass out, you silly one. You don't want to miss out on your steak and shrimp dinner."

Joann giggled.

"I can't believe it! Lord have mercy. Edna, I can't say thank you enough."

"Thank Daddy and Mama when you say your prayers tonight. They made me this way."

"I will definitely thank them."

"Joann, do you want to go with me to church on Sunday?"

"I know you pray a lot, Edna, but I didn't know you had a church to go to."

"I'm embarrassed to say I haven't been to my church since I was eighteen years old."

"Don't be embarrassed. I haven't been to a church at all, but I love and have faith in God, just like you. Going to church doesn't mean you're a Christian, but I would love to go to hear a good sermon."

"Really? Joann, don't you lie to me."

"Edna, you know I wouldn't lie to you."

"I don't know about that."

"I promise I'm telling the truth."

"Okay! I'll pick you up Sunday at 10:00 a.m."

"I will be ready. Edna, the next time we go to church, I'll pick you up in my car."

"Sounds like a good plan."

"I love you, Edna."

"I love you more, my sweet Joann."

"I'm ready for my sirloin, shrimp, and broccoli. I can hardly wait. I can't believe you're going to treat me, but I'm not going to question your kind deed. Let's go right now before you change your mind."

"Ha, ha, ha. Joann, you're a mess."

Listening to God was easy for me to do because I had the right attitude in my heart. One act of kindness changed Joann's perspective on life for the better. Her mental health improved tremendously, and she had a confidence in herself that I hadn't seen in the past. Also, giving made me feel good because I had helped someone. Making a difference in someone's life is rewarding. Life is a special occasion and a special gift from God. The secret to happiness is helping others. The Bible verse Matt 6:19–21 came to my mind: "Lay not up for yourselves treasures upon earth, where moth and rust doth corrupt, and where thieves break through and steal: But lay up for yourselves treasures in heaven, where neither moth nor rust doth corrupt, and where thieves do not break through nor steal." It's amazing how Daddy selected Bible verses that revealed my life's real meaning and purpose. His teaching kept me from wasting years of my life worrying about things that don't matter and helped me trust God to take care of the things that do matter. I'm thankful. My life changed for the better after my revelation in the Internal Medicine Clinic. The change made me feel like a new person, and it made me see the world in a different way. My old desires passed away and new desires came. Many times, I wondered how I had let society redirect me to a world of chaos and confusion when I had been taught and given what was necessary to have a peaceful and fulfilled Christian life. Not only was I taught it, I had lived it. Even though I never came up with an answer to this question, God gave me a second chance to redeem myself, and I won't let Him down. Material things, status, power, and control aren't on my priority list. My priority is pleasing God, not people. He knows I love him, believe in him, and trust him in every part of my life. He's been my Father and Mother, and my everything. He has brought me through a mighty long way, and he never left me during difficult times. I know He will never forsake me because the Bible tells me so: "Be strong and of a good courage, fear not, nor be afraid of them: for the Lord thy God, he it is that doth go with thee; he will not fail thee, nor forsake thee" (Deut 31:6). Loving and having faith in God will give everyone all they need. God's love is mighty sweet and endures forever. God is able to do what others can't do. There is no one like him. I received God's message wholeheartedly, and I'm so happy he saw potential in me.

Endnotes

1. See "Caswell County, North Carolina," https://en.wikipedia.org/wiki/ Caswell_County,_North_Carolina.

2. Don Bolden, "Burlington History," www.ci.burlington.nc.us/62/City-History. See "Burlington, North Carolina," https://en.wikipedia.org/wiki/ Burlington,_North_Carolina.

3. "Man Found Dead Last Night." Burlington Daily Time News, February 23, 1965.

www.ingramcontent.com/pod-product-compliance
Lightning Source LLC
Chambersburg PA
CBHW060348090426
42734CB00011B/2077